LEFT

BIBLE STUDY GUIDE #2

BEHIND

The Antichrist

Neil Wilson and Len Woods

MOODY PUBLISHERS

CHICAGO

© 2003 by Moody Publishers

Written by Neil Wilson and Len Woods.

All rights reserved. No part of this book may be reproduced in any form without permission in writing from the publisher, except in the case of brief quotations embodied in critical articles or reviews.

Material for the Introduction, "How to Study Bible Prophecy," is adapted from the *Tim LaHaye Prophecy Study Bible* © 2001 by AMG Publishers, Chattanooga, Tennessee. All rights reserved. Used by permission.

The "Overview of the End Times" illustration is taken from *Are We Living in the End Times?* (page 99). Copyright © 1999 by Tim LaHaye and Jerry B. Jenkins, Tyndale House Publishers, Wheaton, Illinois. All rights reserved. Used by permission.

All Scripture quotations, unless otherwise indicated, are taken from the *Holy Bible, New Living Translation,* copyright © 1996. Used by permission of Tyndale House Publishers, Wheaton, Illinois 60189. All rights reserved.

Scripture quotations marked KJV are taken from the King James Version.

Scripture quotations marked NASB are taken from the *New American Standard Bible®* Copyright. © The Lockman Foundation 1960, 1962, 1963, 1968, 1971, 1972, 1973, 1975, 1977, 1995. Used by permission.

Scripture quotations marked NIV are taken from the *Holy Bible, New International Version®*. Copyright © 1973, 1978, 1984 by the International Bible Society. Used by permission of Zondervan Bible Publishing House. All rights reserved. The "NIV" and "New International Version" trademarks are registered in the United States Patent and Trademark Office by International Bible Society. Use of either trademark requires the permission of the International Bible Society.

Book quotations taken from *Left Behind* © 1995 by Tim LaHaye and Jerry B. Jenkins; from *The Tribulation Force* ©1996 by Tim LaHaye and Jerry B. Jenkins; from *The Indwelling* © 2000 by Tim LaHaye and Jerry B. Jenkins; from *The Mark* ©2000 by Tim LaHaye and Jerry B. Jenkins; from *Desecration* © 2001 by Tim LaHaye and Jerry B. Jenkins. All titles published by Tyndale House Publishers, Wheaton, Illinois. All rights reserved. Used by permission.

Produced with the assistance of the Livingstone Corporation (www.LivingstoneCorp.com). Project staff includes Len Woods, Neil Wilson, Ashley Taylor, Kirk Luttrell, Mary Horner Collins, Mark Wainwright, Carol Barnstable, and Rosalie Krusemark.

ISBN 0-8024-6464-5

1 3 5 7 9 10 8 6 4 2

Printed in the United States of America

Contents

For the latest information on other Left Behind series and Bible prophecy products, go to www.leftbehind.com. Sign up for a free e-mail update!

Foreword

Tim LaHaye and Jerry B. Jenkins

Jesus said, "Watch and wait!" (Mark 13:32–37).

Even believers looking for the coming of Christ will be surprised at the Rapture. But it will be a delightful surprise—the fulfillment of our deepest longings. One of our goals in the Left Behind novels is to keep others from being surprised in the worst sense—by being caught off guard and left behind.

A large body of literature written in the last half century highlights the growing evidence that Christ's coming is quickly drawing near. We have written several books ourselves seeking to help people understand biblical passages about the end times. *Are We Living in the End Times?* (Tyndale), *The Tim LaHaye Prophecy Study Bible* (AMG), *Will I Be Left Behind?* (Tyndale), and *Perhaps Today* (Tyndale) all were written to help people understand biblical prophecy.

The Left Behind Bible study guide series from Moody Publishers uses material from the novels to illustrate an introduction to Bible prophecy. Authors Neil Wilson and Len Woods emphasize that the Left Behind stories are rooted in biblical themes. They bring together various prophetic passages of Scripture and plenty of thought-provoking questions, with the goal of getting you to live in the light of the imminent return of Christ.

These studies will help you discover what we wanted to show in the novels—that all the historical, technological, and theological pieces of the puzzle recorded in biblical prophecy are more plainly in place for Christ's return now than ever before. Technological advances commonplace today parallel scriptural pictures in such an uncanny way that they allow for prophesied events that even a generation ago seemed impossible.

Biblical prophecy doesn't look nearly as strange anymore. Our intent in the novels was to simply make the truth of the Bible come alive for fiction readers. That many people have been driven back to their Bibles is a wonderful outcome. In your hands is another vehicle that allows you to closely study the Bible texts that thrilled us and served as the basis for the fiction. We encourage you to become a wise student of God's Word and a watchful observer of the times.

Introduction

Neil Wilson and Len Woods

Welcome to this introductory study of end-times prophecy! We pray that you will find these studies helpful, challenging, and encouraging in your walk with Christ.

General interest in prophecy among Christians tends to behave very much like an active volcano. About once in each generation, seismic events in history grab everyone's attention, and the internal pressure to see events from God's point of view causes an eruption of prophetic concerns. Early in our generation toward the end of the 1960s, we experienced just such an eruption with the turbulence surrounding the Vietnam conflict, the heating up of the Cold War, the rise of the Jesus Movement, and the publication of Hal Lindsay's book *The Late Great Planet Earth,* among other things. Larry Norman's song "I Wish We'd All Been Ready" struck a chord of longing and urged our generation to get serious about Jesus. He was coming like a thief in the night. Prophetic students pointed to the rebirth of the nation of Israel and the rapidly closing time period following that event as an indisputable clue to Christ's coming. We tried to get ready—for a while.

Unfortunately, like many examples of public fascination, the wide interest in prophetic issues gradually dwindled to the faithful remnant, who continually read the signs of the times and served the body of Christ with urgent warnings. The volcano seemed to go silent. Here and there, prophecy conferences still gathered. Books were written, papers presented, and even heated arguments raged behind closed doors. The world quickly went on its way to more hopeful outlooks: the fall of the Berlin Wall, the explosive rise of the stock market, and murmured promises that the world might finally be headed toward life as a kinder, gentler place. Continual background trouble was ignored. Even the body of Christ seemed fascinated with herself. The potential of church growth achieved by appealing to seekers and making it very easy to slide into the church created an atmosphere where judgment and Christ's second coming sounded a little harsh and unfriendly. The church became, in many ways, too successful to long for rapture. The distant rumble of the volcano was drowned out by the music of worship that too often sounded a lot more like entertainment than serious consideration of the majesty of God.

The arrival of new centuries and the much rarer dawn of new millenniums have usually created a suspicion that more than just a calendar time line might be coming to an end. Recently, terms like Y2K became shorthand for fearful brooding over the sudden realization that our entire civilization seemed dependent on countless computers remaining sane in spite of a simple change in their internal clocks. Many expected a cyber meltdown. Some predicted a new Dark Ages. Thousands stockpiled food, water, and guns. And most of us wondered what would happen. Christians who knew prophecy simply couldn't see cataclysmic Y2K scenarios indicated in the Bible. Their more or less confident counsel to trust in God's sovereignty was often met with suspicion and derision by those practical believers, whose motto seemed to be "God helps those who help themselves." Y2K caught the church unprepared.

In the predawn jitters of the new millennium, a book was published that seemed to almost instantly grab the imagination of millions. *Left Behind* became plausible fiction. As Tim LaHaye and Jerry Jenkins have repeatedly stated, one of their primary goals was to demonstrate that all the technology was already in place to allow prophetic events to occur that previous generations had found inconceivable. A volcano of interest in prophecy began to rumble. The tremors found their way to the shelves of the largest general market bookstores as millions of the *Left Behind* books left the stores. Many Christians reported surprise over their own lack of understanding of what seems so apparent throughout Scripture. In the years that have followed the publication of the first novel, there has been a healthy movement toward greater acknowledgment that God has a plan for this world, and a deadline is approaching. His Word makes that fact clear, and the events of history are providing confirming echoes.

We trust these studies will tune your heart and mind to the purposes of God. We hope that as a result of studying his Word, you will long for your daily life to harmonize with God's purposes. We pray that you increasingly will be intent on doing what God has set before you, glancing from time to time at the horizon, anticipating your personal encounter with the Lord! May your prayers frequently include, "Maranatha!"—Lord, come quickly!

How to Get the Most from Your Study

Depending on your background and experiences, the Left Behind studies will

- Help you begin to answer some important questions that may have occurred to you as you were reading the Left Behind novels,
- Introduce you to the serious study of biblical prophecy,
- Provide you with a starting point for a personal review of biblical prophecy that you remember hearing about as you were growing up, or
- Offer you a format to use in meeting with others to discuss not only the Left Behind novels but the Bible texts that inspired the stories.

If you are using these studies on your own, you will establish your own pace. A thoughtful consideration of the Bible passages, questions, and quotes from the Left Behind series and other books will require a minimum of an hour for each lesson.

If you will be discussing these lessons as part of a group, make sure you review each lesson on your own. Your efforts in preparation will result in a number of personal benefits:

- You will have thought through some of the most important questions and be less prone to "shallow answers."
- You will have a good sense of the direction of the discussion.
- You will have an opportunity to do some added research if you discover an area or question that you know will be beyond the scope of the group discussion.
- Since a group will probably not be able to cover every question in each lesson because of time constraints, your preparation will allow you to fill in the gaps.

Tools to Use

- Make sure you have a Bible you can read easily.
- Most of the quotes in these studies come from the New Living Translation. If your Bible is a different version, get in the habit of comparing the verses.
- Consider reading some of the excellent books available today for the study of prophecy. You will find helpful suggestions in the endnotes.
- Put some mileage on your pen or pencil. Take time to write out answers to the questions as you prepare each lesson.
- Continually place your life before God. Ultimately, your study of prophecy ought to deepen your awareness of both his sovereignty and compassion. You will appreciate the overwhelming aspects of God's love, mercy, and grace toward you even more as you get a wider view of his grandeur and glory.

Leading a Group Through the Left Behind Studies

Leading a Bible study on prophecy can be daunting to any teacher. When it comes to prophecy, all of us are students; we've all got a lot to learn. Approaching this study as a fresh opportunity to ask questions, to seek the Lord and his Word for answers, and to help others in the process will take the burden of being "the teacher" off your shoulders.

Remember that it's helpful to be confident in what you know as long as you're not confident you know everything. The study of prophecy does bring up many questions for which the most honest answer is, "We don't know." God has, however, given us more information in his Word than he is often given credit for. To use the apostle Paul's language, we may see some things sharply and other things dimly, but that's so much better than being in the dark. Take a careful look at Tim LaHaye's article "How to Study Prophecy," and encourage your group to read it. It provides valuable guidelines as you prepare for these discussions.

No matter the level of knowledge you or your group may have, set your sights on increasing your group's interest in the study of prophecy as well as deepening their commitment to living for Christ. Keep your group focused on the need to know Jesus better. Ultimately, it's hard to get excited about expecting a stranger. The more intimately we get to know Jesus, the more we long to see him. Consider using as a motto for your group the words of Paul, "Yet I am not ashamed, because I know whom I have believed, and am convinced that he is able to guard what I have entrusted to him for that day" (2 Timothy 1:12 NIV).

Prophecy and evangelism travel together. A study like this can provide unexpected opportunities to share the gospel. We tend to think that evangelistic conversations are primarily a backward look with a present application—God has accomplished certain gracious things through Christ and his death and resurrection; therefore, what shall we do today? Prophecy reverses the discussion, creating a forward look with a present application—God promises he will do these things tomorrow; therefore, how shall we live today? Be prayerfully alert to opportunities during and after studies to interact seriously with group members about the state of their souls. Tim LaHaye and Jerry Jenkins have letters from hundreds of readers of the Left Behind series who came to faith in Christ in part as a result of their exposure to prophecy. Pray that God will use your study to accomplish his purposes in others' lives, including yours.

Several Helpful Tools

Bibles: Encourage group members to bring and use their Bibles. We've quoted in the workbook the verses being discussed in each lesson, but having the full context of the verses available to examine is often helpful. We recommend that you have on hand for consultation at least one copy of a trustworthy study Bible that highlights prophetic issues, such as the *Ryrie Study Bible* (Moody Press) or the *Tim LaHaye Prophecy Study Bible* (AMG Publishers).

Bible Concordance and Bible Dictionary: Each of these tools can assist a group in the process of finding specific passages in Scripture or gaining a perspective on a particular biblical theme or word.

Resource Books: The endnotes for each lesson include a number of books from which insightful quotes have been drawn. If members in your group have access to these books, encourage them to make the volumes available for others to read.

Left Behind Novels: Because there are several editions of the books, you may discover some discrepancies in the page listings of the quotes from the novels and the particular books you have. A little search of the pages nearby will usually get you to the right place.

Hints for Group Sessions

1. Encourage participants to review and prepare as much of each lesson as they are able in advance. Remind them it will help the learning process if they have been thinking about the issues and subjects before the session.
2. As you prepare the lessons, decide what questions you will make your focus for discussion. Unless your time is open-ended and your group highly motivated, you will not be able to cover every question adequately in an hour.
3. Only experience with your particular group will give you a sense of how much ground you can cover each session.
4. Consider appointing different group members to ask the questions. That will take the spotlight off you and allow them to participate in a comfortable way.
5. Take time in each session for feedback and questions from the group. These spontaneous reflections will give you a good sense of how much the group is learning, integrating, and being affected by the lessons.

The Place of Prayer

Make it a point to pray with the group and for the group during the study. Use part of your preparation time to bring each person from the group before God in prayer. Open and close each session by asking God, who alone knows the full meaning of every prophecy he has inspired in his Word, to open your hearts and minds to understand and respond in practical, wholehearted ways to the truth of Scripture.

How to Study Bible Prophecy

Tim LaHaye

Prophecy is God's road map to show us where history is going. The Bible's predictions claim literal and specific fulfillments that verify that such prophecies are indeed from God. The key to interpreting Bible prophecy is in discerning what is literal and what is symbolic. Therefore, the best way to avoid confusion in the study of prophetic Scripture is to follow these simple directions:

1. Interpret prophecy literally wherever possible. God meant what he said and said what he meant when he inspired "holy men of God [who] spake as they were moved by the Holy Ghost" (2 Peter 1:21 KJV) to write the Bible. Consequently we can take the Bible literally most of the time. Where God intends for us to interpret symbolically he makes it obvious. One of the reasons the book of Revelation is difficult for some people to understand is that they try to spiritualize the symbols used in the book. However, since many Old Testament prophecies have already been literally fulfilled, such as God turning water to blood (Exodus 4:9; 7:17–21), it should not be difficult to imagine that future prophetic events can and will be literally fulfilled at the appropriate time. Only when symbols or figures of speech make absolutely no literal sense should anything but a literal interpretation be sought.

2. Prophecies concerning Israel and the church should not be transposed. The promises of God to Israel to be fulfilled "in the latter days," particularly those concerning Israel's punishment during the Tribulation, have absolutely nothing to do with the church. The Bible gives specific promises for the church that she will be raptured into heaven before the Tribulation (John 14:2–3; 1 Corinthians 15:51–52; 1 Thessalonians 4:13–18).

3. For symbolic passages, compare Scripture with Scripture. The Bible is not contradictory. Even though written by numerous divinely inspired men over a period of sixteen hundred years, it is supernaturally consistent in its use of terms. For example, the word "beast" is used thirty-four times in Revelation and many other times in Scripture. Daniel explains that the word is symbolic of either a king or kingdom (see Daniel 7–8). By examining the contexts in Revelation and Daniel, you will find that "beast" has the same meaning in both books. Many other symbols used in Revelation are also taken directly from the Old Testament. These include "the tree of life" (Revelation 2:7; 22:2, 14), "the Book of Life" (Revelation 3:5), and Babylon (Revelation 14:8ff.).

Some symbols in Revelation are drawn from other New Testament passages. These include terms such as "the word of God" (1:2, 9ff.), "Son of Man" (1:13; 14:14), "marriage supper" (19:9), "the bride" (21:9; 22:17), "first resurrection" (20:5–6), and "second death" (2:11;

20:6, 14; 21:8). Other symbols in Revelation are explained and identified in their context. For example, "Alpha and Omega" represents Jesus Christ (1:8; 21:6; 22:13); the "seven candle-sticks" (1:13, 20) are the seven churches; the "dragon" is Satan (12:3ff.); and the "man child" is Jesus (12:5, 13).

Though some prophetic passages should be interpreted symbolically, it is important to remember that symbols in the Bible depict real people, things, and events. For example, the "seven candlesticks" in Revelation 1 represent real churches that actually existed when the prophecy was given.

Keeping the three points above in mind will provide you with a confident approach to prophetic Scriptures and guard against a multitude of errors. Allow God's Word always to be your final guide.

(Adapted from the *Tim LaHaye Prophecy Study Bible*, AMG Publishers, used with permission.)

Overview of the End Times

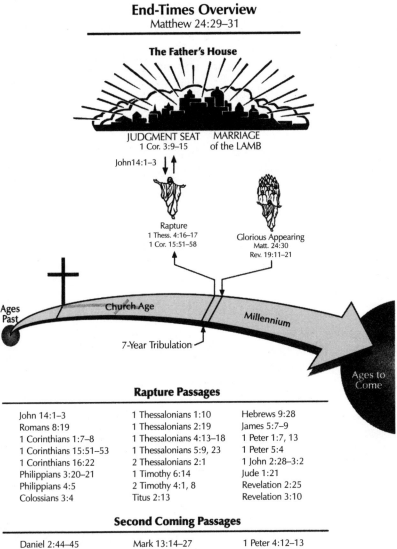

End-Times Overview
Matthew 24:29–31

The Father's House

JUDGMENT SEAT   MARRIAGE
1 Cor. 3:9–15   of the LAMB

John14:1–3

Rapture
1 Thess. 4:16–17
1 Cor. 15:51–58

Glorious Appearing
Matt. 24:30
Rev. 19:11–21

Ages
Past

Church Age

Millennium

7-Year Tribulation

Ages to
Come

Rapture Passages

John 14:1–3	1 Thessalonians 1:10	Hebrews 9:28
Romans 8:19	1 Thessalonians 2:19	James 5:7–9
1 Corinthians 1:7–8	1 Thessalonians 4:13–18	1 Peter 1:7, 13
1 Corinthians 15:51–53	1 Thessalonians 5:9, 23	1 Peter 5:4
1 Corinthians 16:22	2 Thessalonians 2:1	1 John 2:28–3:2
Philippians 3:20–21	1 Timothy 6:14	Jude 1:21
Philippians 4:5	2 Timothy 4:1, 8	Revelation 2:25
Colossians 3:4	Titus 2:13	Revelation 3:10

Second Coming Passages

Daniel 2:44–45	Mark 13:14–27	1 Peter 4:12–13
Daniel 7:9–14	Mark 14:62	2 Peter 3:1–14
Daniel 12:1–3	Luke 21:25–28	Jude 1:14–15
Zechariah 12:10	Acts 1:9–11	Revelation 1:7
Zechariah 14:1–15	Acts 3:19–21	Revelation 19:11–20:6
Matthew 13:41	1 Thessalonians 3:13	Revelation 22:7, 12, 20
Matthew 24:15–31	2 Thessalonians 1:6–10	
Matthew 26:64	2 Thessalonians 2:8	

LEFT

BEHIND

The Antichrist

Lesson 1

The Dragon—the Power Behind the Beast

1. What are some of the common ways Satan is portrayed in pop culture—movies, commercials, cartoons, etc.?

    _____

    _____

    _____

    _____

    _____

> "The biblical portrait of Satan is that he does indeed have great power, but it is always limited by the purposes and plans of God. It is a picture of a proud being who has already been humbled. It is the picture of a being whose greatest asset in his war with us is our own ignorance."[1]
>
> Erwin Lutzer

2. How do you tend to picture Satan? Which of the names in the chart on the next page best captures your mental image of Satan?

    _____

    _____

    _____

    _____

    _____

    _____

Bible Names and Descriptions of Satan

- Lucifer (Isaiah 14:12 KJV)
- Beelzebub (Matthew 12:24–27 NIV)
- the Devil (Matthew 4:1–11)—the word means "slanderer"
- the dragon (Revelation 20:2)
- the Evil One (1 John 5:19)
- that old serpent (Revelation 20:2)
- the tempter (Matthew 4:3 NIV; 1 Thessalonians 3:5)
- the Accuser (Job 1:6; Revelation 12:10)
- the liar (John 8:44)
- the father of lies (John 8:44)
- the murderer (John 8:44)
- the god of this world (2 Corinthians 4:4 NASB)
- the ruler of this world (John 14:30 NIV)
- an angel of light (2 Corinthians 11:14)
- the prince of the power of the air (Ephesians 2:2)

Unfolding the Story

(Left Behind, pp. 419–21)

In the first book of the Left Behind series, the primary focus is on a small group of people who are trying to understand the disappearance of millions from the earth. It isn't long before they realize they have witnessed the event known in the Bible as the Rapture—Christ's coming for his church.

Eventually each of these characters trusts in Christ as Savior and Lord. One of their number, Bruce Barnes, is a pastor with extensive Bible training. A former "make-believer," the post-Rapture Bruce believes passionately in Jesus, and he sees his role as educating others about what the Bible teaches about the end times.

"**IF WHAT YOU'RE SAYING IS TRUE,** there's no room for dabbling."

"You're right. But I've also been thinking about a smaller group within the core. I'm looking for people of unusual intelligence and courage. I don't mean to disparage the sincerity of others in the church, especially those on the leadership team. But some of them are timid, some old, many infirm. I've been praying about sort of an inner circle of people who want to do more than just survive."

"What are you getting at?" Rayford asked. "Going on the offensive?"

"Something like that. It's one thing to hide in here, studying, figuring out what's going on so we can keep from being deceived. It's great to pray for the witnesses springing up out of Israel, and it's nice to know there are other pockets of believers all over the world. But doesn't part of you want to jump into the battle?"

Rayford was intrigued but not sure. Chloe was more eager. "A cause," she said. "Something not just to die for but to live for."

"Yes!"

"A group, a team, a force," Chloe said.

"You've got it. A force."

Chloe's eyes were bright with interest. Rayford loved her youth and her eagerness to commit to a cause that to her was only hours old. "And what is it you call this period?" she asked.

"The Tribulation," Bruce said.

"So your little group inside the group, a sort of Green Berets, would be your Tribulation force."

"Tribulation Force," Bruce said, looking at Rayford and rising to scribble it on his flip chart. "I like it. Make no mistake, it won't be fun. It would be the most dangerous cause a person could ever join. We would study, prepare, and speak out. When it becomes obvious who the Antichrist is, the false prophet, the evil, counterfeit religion, we'll have to oppose them, speak out against them. We would be targeted. Christians content to hide in basements with their Bibles might escape everything but earthquakes and wars, but we will be vulnerable to everything.

"There will come a time, Chloe, that followers of Antichrist will be required to bear the sign of the beast. There are all kinds of theories on what form that might take, from a tattoo to a stamp on the forehead that might be detected only under infrared light. But obviously we would refuse to bear that mark. That very act of defiance will be a mark in itself. We will be the naked ones, the ones void of the protection of belonging to the majority. You still want to be part of the Tribulation Force?"

Rayford nodded and smiled at his daughter's firm reply. "I wouldn't miss it."

3. In the passage just cited, the members of the so-called Tribulation Force seem to be steeling themselves for trouble. Why?

    _____

    _____

    _____

    _____

    _____

4. How well do you think they *really* understand the great evil they will eventually face?

    _____

    _____

    _____

    _____

Back to Reality

The Rapture has not yet occurred ("Come quickly, Lord Jesus!"), and we are not facing the great horrors of the Tribulation period (thank God!). But all evidence suggests we could very well be living in the era that will see these cataclysmic events.

The late Dr. John Walvoord, former president of Dallas Theological Seminary and long considered one of the most knowledgeable prophecy scholars in the world, said before his death in 2002: "I have been studying prophecy for many years, and while I do not believe it is possible to set dates for the Lord's return, I do sense in the world today an unprecedented time of world crises that can be interpreted as being preparatory for the coming of the Lord. If there ever was a time when Christians should live every day as though Christ could come at any time, it is today."[2]

5. Do you agree with Dr. Walvoord? Why or why not? Do you personally think the world is becoming more corrupt, more evil with each passing year? Why or why not? What evidence would you cite to bolster your argument?

    _____

    _____

_____

_____

_____

6. In trying to explain the existence of evil in the world, how much blame do you put on the devil? Why?

_____

_____

_____

_____

_____

7. What would likely happen if a respected national figure went on television and spoke matter-of-factly of a deep belief in a real personality named Satan?

_____

_____

_____

_____

Understanding the Word

The media and educational elite of our generation might scoff at serious talk of the devil and at the belief in a coming battle between good and evil, God and Satan, but the Bible speaks frankly of such realities. The Old Testament prophet Isaiah gives us insight into the origins of Satan:

> *How you are fallen from heaven, O shining star, son of the morning! You have been thrown down to the earth, you who destroyed the nations of the world. For you said to yourself, "I will ascend to heaven and set my throne above God's stars. I will preside on the mountain of the gods far away in the north. I will climb to the highest heavens and be like the Most High." But instead, you will be brought down to the place of the dead, down*

to its lowest depths. Everyone there will stare at you and ask, "Can this be the one who shook the earth and the kingdoms of the world? Is this the one who destroyed the world and made it into a wilderness?" (Isaiah 14:12–17)

8. What sort of picture does this passage paint of Satan's beginnings?

    _____

    _____

    _____

    _____

9. According to these verses, what prompted this *creature* we know as the devil to rebel against almighty God, the *Creator* of all?

    _____

    _____

    _____

    _____

    _____

Revelation 12 shows us Satan's murderous fury against God and everything associated with heaven. It is a glimpse of a cosmic battle that will break out halfway through the tribulation:

> *Then I witnessed in heaven an event of great significance. I saw a woman clothed with the sun, with the moon beneath her feet, and a crown of twelve stars on her head. She was pregnant, and she cried out in the pain of labor as she awaited her delivery.*
>
> *Suddenly, I witnessed in heaven another significant event. I saw a large red dragon with seven heads and ten horns, with seven crowns on his heads. His tail dragged down one-third of the stars, which he threw to the earth. He stood before the woman as she was about to give birth to her child, ready to devour the baby as soon as it was born.*
>
> *She gave birth to a boy who was to rule all nations with an iron rod. And the child was snatched away from the dragon and was caught up to God and to his throne. And the woman fled into the wilderness, where God had prepared a place to give her care for 1,260 days.*
>
> *Then there was war in heaven. Michael and the angels under his command fought the dragon and his angels. And the dragon lost the battle and was forced out of heaven. This*

great dragon—the ancient serpent called the Devil, or Satan, the one deceiving the whole world—was thrown down to the earth with all his angels.

Then I heard a loud voice shouting across the heavens, "It has happened at last—the salvation and power and kingdom of our God, and the authority of his Christ! For the Accuser has been thrown down to earth—the one who accused our brothers and sisters before our God day and night. And they have defeated him because of the blood of the Lamb and because of their testimony. And they were not afraid to die. Rejoice, O heavens! And you who live in the heavens, rejoice! But terror will come on the earth and the sea. For the Devil has come down to you in great anger, and he knows that he has little time."

And when the dragon realized that he had been thrown down to the earth, he pursued the woman who had given birth to the child. But she was given two wings like those of a great eagle. This allowed her to fly to a place prepared for her in the wilderness, where she would be cared for and protected from the dragon for a time, times, and half a time.

Then the dragon tried to drown the woman with a flood of water that flowed from its mouth. But the earth helped her by opening its mouth and swallowing the river that gushed out from the mouth of the dragon. Then the dragon became angry at the woman, and he declared war against the rest of her children—all who keep God's commandments and confess that they belong to Jesus. (Revelation 12:1–17)

10. What adjectives and phrases are used to describe the dragon? What verbs describe his activity?

   _____

   _____

   _____

   _____

   _____

11. If the dragon represents Satan, the woman in this vision symbolizes the nation of Israel, and the child is Christ, what does this passage say that Jews living in the Tribulation can expect?

   _____

   _____

   _____

   _____

WHAT DOES THE DEVIL DO?

- Tries to thwart and/or subvert God's plan (Matthew 4:1–11; 16:23)
- Blinds the minds of unbelievers so that they will not accept the gospel (2 Corinthians 4:4)
- Deceives nations (Revelation 20:3)
- Keeps God's Word from taking root and bearing fruit (Luke 8:12)
- Hinders the work of God (1 Thessalonians 2:18)
- Tempts toward immorality (1 Corinthians 7:5)
- Accuses and slanders believers (Revelation 12:10)
- Incites persecution against believers (Revelation 2:10)
- Commands a host of demonic powers (Ephesians 6:11–12)
- Tempts believers to lie (Acts 5:3)
- Tries to steal the worship and honor that belongs rightfully only to God (Revelation 13:12)

12. Which of the devil's activities (listed in "What Does the Devil Do?") causes you the most concern? Why?

_____

_____

_____

_____

_____

_____

13. What are some ways that you may have been the subject of demonic or devilish attack? (Again, refer to the list.)

_____

_____

_____

_____

_____

_____

_____

"The Word of God tells us he [Satan] is an immensely powerful, unutterably malevolent spirit being who lives to murder and deceive mankind. He will do everything he can to usurp the worship and glory that belong to God alone—and we do mean 'everything.'" [3]

Tim LaHaye and Jerry Jenkins

Finding the Connection

In the Left Behind series, the Tribulation Force hungrily engages in a careful study of Scripture. Led by pastor Bruce Barnes, Rayford and Chloe Steele and Buck Williams realize that their enemy is real, and that the battle in front of them is one of cosmic proportions and eternal ramifications.

These fledgling believers do their best to prepare for the hard times ahead by poring over God's truth (so they will have an anchor in the midst of their fiery trials) and by praying continuously.

14. Spiritually speaking, do you sense that you are actually living in the middle of a cosmic battleground? Or on most days, do you live as though the war between good and evil is over? Explain.

_____

_____

_____

_____

15. Ephesians 6:10–11 warns us:

A final word: Be strong with the Lord's mighty power. Put on all of God's armor so that you will be able to stand firm against all strategies and tricks of the Devil.

What does this passage reveal about the devil? What does it tell us about God? What is our responsibility?

_____

_____

_____

_____

_____

_____

"We believe this great conflict [the one described in Revelation 12] occurs at the midpoint of the Tribulation. After Satan is defeated, evicted from heaven, and banished to earth, he personally indwells the Antichrist and through 'the Beast' receives the worship he has always lusted after. This begins with the 'abomination that causes desolation,' when the Antichrist defiles the rebuilt temple by taking his seat there, declaring himself to be god. This event, as we have seen, triggers the 'Great Tribulation' and the outpouring of the wrath of the Lamb. Satan knows that at this point he has but three and a half years before his incarceration and final doom, and that certain knowledge fills him with 'great wrath.'

"Is it any wonder the second half of the Tribulation will be the most awful period in the history of humankind?"[4]

Tim LaHaye and Jerry B. Jenkins

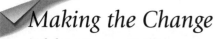# Making the Change

(_Tribulation Force_, pp. 38–39)

"So what? Big deal? What difference does all this make in my life?"

Those are wise and reasonable questions. We should _always_ ask these kinds of application questions when confronted with the trustworthy and true Word of God. Otherwise Bible study becomes an end in itself, rather than a means to a greater end—a transformed life.

The second novel of the Left Behind series features the following exchange between Rayford Steele and his college-aged daughter, Chloe:

> "SITTING HERE TALKING about my love life, or lack of it, seems pretty juvenile at this point in history, don't you think? It's not like there's nothing to fill my time even if I don't go back to school. I want to memorize Ezekiel, Daniel, and Revelation for starters."
>
> Rayford laughed. "You're kidding!"
>
> "Of course! But you know what I mean, Dad? I never would've dreamed the Bible would even interest me, but now I'm reading it like there's no tomorrow."
>
> Rayford fell silent, and he could tell Chloe was struck by her own unintentional

irony. "I am too," he said. "I already know more about end-times prophecy than I ever knew existed. We're living it, right here, right now. There aren't many tomorrows left, are there?"

16. It took major, life-altering, world-shaking events for the members of the Tribulation Force to get serious about God. What will it take for you? If all that we are studying here is true, do your priorities need to be adjusted? How? What are you doing that you need to stop doing? What do you need to begin doing that you're not doing?

_____

_____

_____

_____

_____

_____

_____

_____

Renowned British author and Christian apologist C. S. Lewis once noted that there are two mistakes people can make when considering the subject of the devil. Either we dismiss him completely and do not think about him at all, or we obsess over him and see him hiding behind every bush. Both mind-sets are flawed.[5]

Pursuing the Truth

James 4:4–8 says:

> You adulterers! Don't you realize that friendship with this world makes you an enemy of God? I say it again, that if your aim is to enjoy this world, you can't be a friend of God. What do you think the Scriptures mean when they say that the Holy Spirit, whom God has placed within us, jealously longs for us to be faithful? He gives us more and more strength to stand against such evil desires. As the Scriptures say, "God sets himself against the proud, but he shows favor to the humble."
>
> So humble yourselves before God. Resist the Devil, and he will flee from you. Draw close to God, and God will draw close to you.

17. How does a Christian "resist the devil"?

_____

_____

_____

_____

_____

18. If one of Satan's primary goals is to "deceive," how does he pull this off where Christians are concerned? In other words, what distorted thoughts about God, ourselves, or life sometimes cloud our thinking?

_____

_____

_____

_____

_____

_____

19. How can being a student of God's Word guard us against the devil's lies?

_____

_____

_____

_____

_____

_____

"Three times in the book of Revelation [Satan] is 'thrown down.' . . . Each round is more humiliating and tortuous than the preceding one. First, he is thrown from heaven to earth (Revelation 12:9); then he is thrown from earth into the Abyss (20:3); and finally he is thrown into the lake of fire (20:10). The proud being who thought it would be to his advantage to stand against God will have to endure an eternity of humiliation." [6]

Erwin Lutzer

20. Does it strike you as just a little bit odd that a huge percentage of Christians—people who claim to base their lives and eternities on the Bible—have never even read the whole Bible? Why do you think this is so?

_____

_____

_____

_____

_____

_____

21. For another peek at Satan's original sin of rebellion against God, read Ezekiel 28:12–17. What stands out the most to you about Satan's beginning status and the end that awaits him?

_____

_____

_____

_____

_____

_____

ALL'S WELL THAT ENDS WELL

"At the very end of the Tribulation Jesus returns to earth in the Glorious Appearing, defeats the armies of the Antichrist and the kings of the earth, and directs a mighty angel to seize Satan and bind him in the bottomless pit for a thousand years (Revelation 20:1–3). At the end of that period, Satan is released for a little while, that he might go throughout the earth and deceive the unbelievers who have grown up at the end of the Millennium. These young people try to attack the Holy City, but fire from heaven destroys them all. And then, at long last, the devil himself—the deceiver, the tempter, the accuser, the liar, the murderer, the god of this world—is hurled into the lake of fire, where he will be tormented day and night forever and ever (Revelation 20:7–10).

Such is the end of Satan, . . . not with a bang, but with a splash." [7]

Tim LaHaye and Jerry B. Jenkins

Lesson in Review . . .

- The Antichrist of the end times is energized by none other than Satan himself.
- As he has done from ages past, the devil (a.k.a., the dragon) will work through the Antichrist to try to gain the glory and honor and worship reserved for God himself.
- At the end of the Tribulation, Jesus will return to earth, defeat the armies of Antichrist, seize and bind Satan, and cast him into the bottomless pit for the duration of the Millennium.
- Following one final rebellion, Satan will be hurled into the lake of fire (i.e., hell) forever.

LEFT
BEHIND

The Antichrist

Lesson 2
The Rise of the Beast

1. What qualities do you look for in a leader?

   _____

   _____

   _____

   _____

2. How would you describe what you consider the most serious way in which a leader can fail his or her followers?

   _____

   _____

   _____

   _____

Unfolding the Story
(*Left Behind*, pp. 413–15)

Book one of the Left Behind series features a world reeling from the sudden disappearance of millions. But then an even more surprising series of events catapults Nicolae Carpathia, an unknown politician from Romania, onto the world's center stage.

> **THE CNN REPORTER CONTINUED,** "In only a matter of hours, every request Carpathia had outlined in an early morning press conference was moved as official business, voted upon, and ratified by the body. Within a year the United Nations

headquarters will move to New Babylon. The makeup of the Security Council will change to ten permanent members within the month, and a press conference is expected Monday morning in which Carpathia will introduce several of his personal choices for delegates to that body.

"There is no guarantee, of course, that even member nations will unanimously go along with the move to destroy ninety percent of their military strength and turn over the remaining ten percent to the U.N. But several ambassadors expressed their confidence 'in equipping and arming an international peacekeeping body with a thorough-going pacifist and committed disarmament activist as its head.' Carpathia himself was quoted as saying, 'The U.N. will not need its military might if no one else has any, and I look forward to the day when even the U.N. disarms.'

"Also coming out of today's meetings was the announcement of a seven-year pact between U.N. members and Israel, guaranteeing its borders and promising peace. In exchange, Israel will allow the U.N. to selectively franchise the use of the fertilizer formula, developed by Nobel prizewinner Dr. Chaim Rosenzweig, which makes desert sands tillable and has made Israel a top exporter."

Buck stared as CNN broadcast Rosenzweig's excitement and unequivocal endorsement of Carpathia. The news also carried a report that Carpathia had asked several international groups already in New York for upcoming meetings to get together this weekend to hammer out proposals, resolutions, and accords. "I urge them to move quickly toward anything that contributes to world peace and a sense of global unity."

A reporter asked Carpathia if that included plans for one world religion and eventually one world government. His response: "I can think of little more encouraging than the religions of the world finally cooperating. Some of the worst examples of discord and infighting have been between groups whose overall mission is love among people. Every devotee of pure religion should welcome this potential. The day of hatred is past. Lovers of humankind are uniting."

The CNN anchor continued, "Among other developments today, there are rumors of the organization of groups espousing one world government. Carpathia was asked if he aspired to a position of leadership in such an organization."

Carpathia looked directly into the network pool camera and with moist eyes and thick voice said, "I am overwhelmed to have been asked to serve as secretary-general of the United Nations. I aspire to nothing else. While the idea of one world government resonates deep within me, I can say only that there are many more qualified candidates to lead such a venture. It would be my privilege to serve in any way I am asked, and while I do not see myself in the leadership role, I will commit the resources of the United Nations to such an effort, if asked."

Smooth, Buck thought, his mind reeling. As commentators and world leaders endorsed one world currency, one language, and even the largesse of Carpathia expressing his support for the rebuilding of the temple in Israel, the staff of *Global Weekly's* Chicago bureau seemed in a mood to party. "This is the first time in years I've felt optimistic about society," one reporter said.

3. In the Left Behind books, we meet Nicolae Carpathia, who rises meteorically to world power. What qualities does this young Romanian have that seem to account for this sudden popularity (see *Left Behind,* chapter 15)?

    _____

    _____

    _____

    _____

    _____

4. Who in your opinion are the top two or three leaders in the world today? (Note: Don't just think in terms of political leaders. Consider leaders in other fields too—academic, spiritual, technological, commercial, etc.). Why?

    _____

    _____

    _____

    _____

    _____

Back to Reality

"Desperate times call for desperate measures," the old saying goes. And so it isn't difficult at all to imagine panicky world leaders (and their frantic populations) laying aside their differences, giving up their autonomy, and pledging allegiance to someone who seems to have all the answers.

5. The United Nations (at least in a diplomatic sense) seems to be gaining more and more clout. Individual nations are discouraged from acting militarily and/or economically without the support and approval from other countries. Do you think, as the novels suggest, the U.N. could be the vehicle for the rise of the Antichrist? Explain.

_____

_____

_____

_____

_____

6. Do most people prefer the promise of safety and security or the riskiness of freedom? Why do you think?

_____

_____

_____

_____

7. As you consider the arenas of science, trade, banking, and education; as you think about trends like globalism, the environmental movement, and pacifism; as you look at the increasing number of international treaties and agreements being signed, what concerns, if any, do you have about these developments?

_____

_____

_____

_____

Understanding the Word

The Left Behind series, in addition to being a pulse-pounding adventure, pulls back the curtain to show how events predicted in the Bible long ago might unfold in the very near future. In the sixth century B.C., the Jewish prophet Daniel saw visions of the end times and of the rise of a world leader not unlike Nicolae Carpathia:

Then in my vision that night, I saw a fourth beast, terrifying, dreadful, and very strong. It devoured and crushed its victims with huge iron teeth and trampled what was left beneath its feet. It was different from any of the other beasts, and it had ten horns. As I was look-ing at the horns, suddenly another small horn appeared among them. Three of the first horns were wrenched out, roots and all, to make room for it. This little horn had eyes like human eyes and a mouth that was boasting arrogantly. . . .

As I watched, this horn was waging war against the holy people and was defeating them. . . . He will defy the Most High and wear down the holy people of the Most High. He will try to change their sacred festivals and laws, and they will be placed under his control for a time, times, and half a time. But then the court will pass judgment, and all his power will be taken away and completely destroyed. (Daniel 7:7–8, 21, 25–26)

8. Conservative Bible scholars agree this "little horn" of Daniel's prophecy is the beast (i.e., Antichrist) described in Revelation 13. How is he depicted by Daniel?

_____

_____

_____

An Antichrist by Any Other Name . . .
- little horn (Daniel 7:11)
- man of lawlessness (2 Thessalonians 2:3)
- the son of perdition (2 Thessalonians 2:3 KJV)
- the man doomed to destruction (2 Thessalonians 2:3 NIV)
- the beast (Revelation 13:1–18; 14:9–11; 15:2)
- evil man (2 Thessalonians 2:9)

God revealed to Daniel a great deal more about the leader who would eventually rise to power as history reached its anticlimax:

The king will do as he pleases, exalting himself and claiming to be greater than every god there is, even blaspheming the God of gods. He will succeed—until the time of wrath is completed. For what has been determined will surely take place. He will have no regard for the gods of his ancestors, or for the god beloved of women, or for any other god, for he will boast that he is greater than them all. Instead of these, he will worship the god of fortresses—a god his ancestors never knew—and lavish on him gold, silver, precious stones, and costly gifts. Claiming this foreign god's help, he will attack the strongest fortresses. He will honor those who submit to him, appointing them to positions of authority and dividing the land among them as their reward.

Then at the time of the end, the king of the south will attack him, and the king of the north will storm out against him with chariots, cavalry, and a vast navy. He will invade various lands and sweep through them like a flood. He will enter the glorious land of Israel, and many nations will fall, but Moab, Edom, and the best part of Ammon will escape. He will conquer many countries, and Egypt will not escape. He will gain control over the gold, silver, and treasures of Egypt, and the Libyans and Ethiopians will be his servants.

But then news from the east and the north will alarm him, and he will set out in great anger to destroy many as he goes. He will halt between the glorious holy mountain and the sea and will pitch his royal tents there, but while he is there, his time will suddenly run out, and there will be no one to help him. (Daniel 11:36–45)

9. What additional details about the Antichrist are revealed in this passage?

    _____

    _____

    _____

10. How successful will the beast (i.e., Antichrist) be in consolidating power, riches, worship? What is the destiny of the Antichrist?

    _____

    _____

    _____

    _____

A REVIVED ROMAN EMPIRE?

"The old Roman Empire was divided and eventually fell apart in fulfillment of biblical prophecy. The ultimate result of this breakup was the formation of the various nations in Europe, . . . but the Bible also prophesies a future revival of the Roman Empire.

"For many years skeptics dismissed this prophecy because for hundreds of years Europe has been divided into sovereign kingdoms and nations that fought each other to maintain their independence and/or conquer and rule their neighbors.

"But all of a sudden in 1989, the Berlin Wall fell and Germany was reunified. And then the European economic union emerged, and now we have something called the Euro, a common currency to be used over most of Europe. The nations in the union have surrendered their currencies to unite under one standard. Suddenly, the picture of a reunified Europe is taking shape.

"The Bible says this process will ultimately come down to a ten-nation alliance, out of which the little horn, or Antichrist, will emerge. Horns are a symbol of power in the Bible, so his power will be small at first. I take it the world won't notice the Antichrist when he first begins making his move."[1]

Tony Evans

Finding the Connection

(*Left Behind*, pp. 323–24)

In the Left Behind series, within two weeks of the vanishings (the Rapture), Nicolae Carpathia, a charismatic leader from Romania, is swept to international power as secretary-general of the United Nations. His pledge is to unite a troubled world into one peaceful village.

One scene features ace reporter Buck Williams surprised to learn that his boss, Steve Plank, is leaving his position at the *Global Weekly* to become the spokesman for this rising world politico.

"I STILL CAN'T BELIEVE you'd leave to become a press secretary, Steve. Even for Nicolae Carpathia."

"Do you know what's in store for him, Buck?"

"A little."

"There's a sea of power and influence and money behind him that will propel him to world prominence so quick it'll make everyone's head spin."

"Listen to yourself. You're supposed to be a journalist."

"I hear myself, Buck. I wouldn't feel this way about anybody else. No U.S. president could turn my head like this, no U.N. secretary-general."

"You think he'll be bigger than that."

"The world is ready for Carpathia, Buck. You were there Monday. You saw it. You heard it. Have you ever met anyone like him?"

"No."

"You never will again, either. If you ask me, Romania is too small for him. Europe is too small for him. The U.N. is too small for him."

"What's he gonna be, Steve, king of the world?"

Steve laughed. "That won't be the title, but don't put it past him. The best part is, he's not even aware of his own presence. He doesn't seek these roles. They are thrust upon him because of his intellect, his power, his passion. . . . I'm sure I'm sitting on one of the greatest rises to power of anyone in history. Maybe the greatest."

11. Consider how the citizens of the United States rallied (almost unanimously) around a relatively untested President George W. Bush following the terrorist attack of 9-11. How far-fetched is it to imagine that in a time of worldwide crisis, the peoples of the earth would eagerly pledge allegiance to a brilliant, smooth-talking, telegenic personality?

_____

_____

_____

_____

12. Do you think the Antichrist could be alive today? Why or why not?

_____

_____

_____

_____

_____

13. Why is discernment such an important quality to develop in all areas of life, but particularly when it comes to spiritual matters?

_____

_____

_____

_____

Making the Change

Perhaps you are a Christian and you are thinking: "This is all well and good. It is helpful and interesting to know about all these events that will unfold during the Tribulation. However, *I won't be here!* Since I'll be raptured with all the other believers in Jesus, I don't have to worry about being deceived by the Antichrist!"

Consider this passage from the apostle John:

> *Dear children, the last hour is here. You have heard that the Antichrist is coming, and already many such antichrists have appeared. From this we know that the end of the world has come. These people left our churches because they never really belonged with us; otherwise they would have stayed with us. When they left us, it proved that they do not belong with us. But you are not like that, for the Holy Spirit has come upon you, and all of you know the truth. So I am writing to you not because you don't know the truth but because you know the difference between truth and falsehood. And who is the great liar? The one who says that Jesus is not the Christ. Such people are antichrists, for they have denied the Father and the Son. . . .*
>
> *I have written these things to you because you need to be aware of those who want to lead you astray. But you have received the Holy Spirit, and he lives within you, so you don't need anyone to teach you what is true. For the Spirit teaches you all things, and what he teaches is true—it is not a lie. So continue in what he has taught you, and continue to live in Christ.* (1 John 2:18–27)

The apostle was making the point, almost two thousand years ago, that a spirit of deception is always prevalent in the world. Even though the Antichrist (capital A) hasn't yet appeared, there are other antichrists (lowercase a) bent on leading the people of God astray.

14. What are some false teachings or philosophies that permeate our culture today that would fall under the category of antichrist teachings?

_____

_____

_____

_____

_____

15. What is the best way for a Christian to avoid being swept up into false doctrine?

_____

_____

_____

16. How can leaders dupe us? In what ways have you experienced being terribly disappointed by a leader (political, moral, etc.)?

_____

_____

_____

_____

Pursuing the Truth

The following passage from the New Testament is one of the key texts for understanding the person and plan of the Antichrist.

> And now, brothers and sisters, let us tell you about the coming again of our Lord Jesus Christ and how we will be gathered together to meet him. Please don't be so easily shaken and troubled by those who say that the day of the Lord has already begun. Even if they claim to have had a vision, a revelation, or a letter supposedly from us, don't believe them. Don't be fooled by what they say.
>
> For that day will not come until there is a great rebellion against God and the man of lawlessness is revealed—the one who brings destruction. He will exalt himself and defy every god there is and tear down every object of adoration and worship. He will position himself in the temple of God, claiming that he himself is God. Don't you remember that I told you this when I was with you? And you know what is holding him back, for he can be revealed only when his time comes.
>
> For this lawlessness is already at work secretly, and it will remain secret until the one who is holding it back steps out of the way. Then the man of lawlessness will be revealed, whom the Lord Jesus will consume with the breath of his mouth and destroy by the splendor of his coming. This evil man will come to do the work of Satan with counterfeit power and signs and miracles. He will use every kind of wicked deception to fool those who are on their way to destruction because they refuse to believe the truth that would save them.

So God will send great deception upon them, and they will believe all these lies. Then they will be condemned for not believing the truth and for enjoying the evil they do. (2 Thessalonians 2:1–12)

17. According to this passage from the inspired pen of Paul, the Antichrist will institute a new religious system and claim to be God. How will people living at that time fall for such a lie?

_____

_____

_____

_____

"Satan doesn't mind religion as long as he can use it. But his ultimate purpose is to wipe out all vestiges of worship to God and usurp God's place on the throne. The Great Tribulation is the closest Satan will come to his age-old desire, because for that brief period he will be the object of people's worship through the Antichrist." [2]

Tony Evans

18. Politicians promise many things, but imagine a dashing and charming world leader who pledged (and could seemingly deliver!) world peace and economic prosperity. Do you think people would follow him? Why?

_____

_____

_____

_____

19. Who or what restrains or "holds back" the rampant lawlessness and deception of the beast?

_____

_____

_____

_____

"By the time the Antichrist appears, the world will be ready to deify a leader if he appears to have what it takes to unite the world and bring in an era of peace. It is not enough for Satan to inhabit a man who will claim to be God. The master deceiver will actually try to duplicate the three members of the Trinity. These three personalities will do their best to try to confuse the world by pretending to be the true and living God."[3]

Erwin Lutzer

Lesson in Review . . .

- Following the Rapture, the earth will be filled with chaos and uncertainty.
- In accordance with biblical prophecy, a charismatic, peace-preaching leader—inspired and empowered by Satan himself—will emerge.
- This leader—called variously the beast, the Antichrist, or the man of sin—will be against Christ and will seek to undermine and even imitate him.
- The Antichrist will deceive the world and gain control of all who do not turn to Christ.

"Once the Antichrist has total political and religious control, he will be ready for his unveiling, the Great Tribulation, when Satan pulls off the mask and shows the world his true nature. It is as though God is saying, 'You wanted a world without Me. Now you have it. Satan, the earth is yours.' "[4]

Tony Evans

LEFT

BIBLE STUDY GUIDE # 2

BEHIND

The Antichrist

Lesson 3
The Character of the Beast

1. When you think of evil personified, what names (villains, mass murderers, etc.) come to mind?

_____

_____

_____

_____

_____

_____

Unfolding the Story
(*Left Behind*, pp. 425–28, 457–58)

Near the conclusion of book one of the Left Behind series, reporter Buck Williams has been invited to meet with the mysterious Nicolae Carpathia, suddenly the world's most powerful and popular leader. Filled with spiritual questions, Buck visits minister Bruce Barnes:

> BRUCE SPENT THE NEXT SEVERAL HOURS giving Buck a crash course in prophecy and the end times. Buck had heard much of the information about the Rapture and the two witnesses, and he had picked up snippets about the Antichrist. But when Bruce got to the parts about the great one-world religion that would spring up, the lying, so-called peacemaker who would bring bloodshed through war, the Antichrist who would divide the world into ten kingdoms, Buck's blood ran cold. He fell silent, no longer peppering Bruce with questions or comments. He scribbled notes as fast as he could.

Did he dare tell this unpretentious man that he believed Nicolae Carpathia could be the very man the Scriptures talked about? Could all this be coincidental? His fingers began to shake when Bruce told of the prediction of a seven-year pact between Antichrist and Israel, the rebuilding of the temple, and even of Babylon becoming headquarters for a new world order. . . .

"You think Carpathia is the Antichrist?"

"I don't see how I could come to any other conclusion."

"But I really believed in the guy."

"Why not? Most of us did. Self-effacing, interested in the welfare of the people, humble, not looking for power or leadership. But the Antichrist is a deceiver. And he has the power to control men's minds. He can make people see lies as truth. . . . If he is the evil one the Bible speaks of, there is little he does not have the power to do."

Buck leaves and cannot stop thinking about Bruce's sobering words (and all the other events that have transpired over the previous weeks). Just before his meeting with Carpathia, a very anxious and desperate Buck places his trust in Christ. He becomes a believer and follower of Jesus. Then he enters the room and after some formal introductions witnesses the true nature of Nicolae.

CARPATHIA WAS IN NO HURRY. "I am going to kill Mr. Stonagal [his wealthy benefactor] with a painless hollow-point round to the brain which he will neither hear nor feel. The rest of us will experience some ringing in our ears. This will be instructive for you all. You will understand cognitively that I am in charge, that I fear no man, and that no one can oppose me. . . .

"When Mr. Stonagal is dead, I will tell you what you will remember. And lest anyone feel I have not been fair, let me not neglect to add that more than gore will wind up on Mr. Todd-Cothran's suit [a powerful British financier]. A high-velocity bullet at this range will also kill him, which, as you know, Mr. Williams, is something I promised you I would deal with in due time."

Todd-Cothran opened his eyes at that news, and Buck heard himself shouting, "No!" as Carpathia pulled the trigger. The blast rattled the windows and even the door. Stonagal's head crashed into the toppling Todd-Cothran, and both were plainly dead before their entwined bodies reached the floor. . . .

"What we have just witnessed here," he said kindly, as if speaking to children, "was a horrible, tragic end to two otherwise extravagantly productive lives. These men were two I respected and admired more than any others in the world. What compelled Mr. Stonagal to rush the guard, disarm him, take his own life and that of his British colleague, I do not know and may never fully understand."

Buck fought within himself to keep his sanity, to maintain a clear mind, to—as his boss told him on the way in—"remember everything."

2. What strikes you most about Nicolae's personality? What five adjectives would you use to describe him?

_____

_____

_____

_____

_____

_____

_____

3. Shortly after the incident described above, Nicolae, in effect, "brainwashes" the witnesses to this double murder. The result is that they remember this event as a murder-suicide (with Stonagal as the perpetrator). Furthermore, no one recalls Buck's presence in the room. How does this eerie power affect Buck?

_____

_____

_____

_____

_____

Back to Reality

Though we are living on this side of the Rapture, and though the Antichrist has not yet made his appearance and seized control of the world, we see the spirit of this murderous liar running rampant in *our* times.

4. Try an experiment. The next time you watch a nightly newscast or read the daily newspaper, count the reports of raw brutality and violence. There was a time when people were

shocked and outraged by senseless murders. Now we seem numbed by the sheer number of them. Why?

_____

_____

_____

_____

_____

_____

5. Think about some of the great ironies of our day:
    - Laws that stringently protect bald eagles and manatees but that allow unborn children to be dismembered in their mother's wombs.
    - A society that refuses to champion sexual abstinence and then wrings its hands at an epidemic of incurable STDs.
    - A renegade judicial system issuing a steady stream of rulings that contradict the convictions and writings of our Founding Fathers.
    - Hospitals where doctors work feverishly to save lives in one room, while colleagues take life in another—endangering both the very young and the very old.
    - An educational establishment that promotes both evolutionary theory and homosexuality as normal and good (even though homosexuality, strictly practiced, would lead to the extinction of our race).

    How many other societal inconsistencies like these can you list?

    _____

    _____

    _____

    _____

    _____

    _____

6. We live in a society that prides itself in being pluralistic—filled with groups and people who "agree to disagree." How clearly does that description fit our culture? At what point do you think that a society trying to contain such shocking contradictions as listed above can no longer keep from shattering from the pressure?

_____

_____

_____

_____

_____

_____

7. What should be the role of Christians living in an era where many "call evil good and good evil" (Isaiah 5:20 NIV)?

_____

_____

_____

_____

_____

_____

Understanding the Word

You do not have to be a Bible professor to see the nature of the Evil One. His true colors are already evident to all who are willing to look. And when he makes his grand appearance on earth during the last days as the Antichrist, his character will be clearly seen. Note carefully each of the traits listed below, drawn from prophecies that clearly depict his abject evil.

He is powerful.

This beast looked like a leopard, but it had bear's feet and a lion's mouth! And the dragon gave him his own power and throne and great authority. (Revelation 13:2)

Then the beast was allowed to speak great blasphemies against God. And he was given authority to do what he wanted for forty-two months. (Revelation 13:5)

8. With the church (and thus the Holy Spirit) removed from the earth, with Satan's full power behind him, and with divine permission to basically do what he wants, how do you envision Satan using his power during the Tribulation period?

_____

_____

_____

_____

_____

_____

He is deceitful (Revelation 13:14; 20:3, 8).

> *This evil man will come to do the work of Satan with counterfeit power and signs and miracles. He will use every kind of wicked deception to fool those who are on their way to destruction because they refuse to believe the truth that would save them. So God will send great deception upon them, and they will believe all these lies. Then they will be condemned for not believing the truth and for enjoying the evil they do.* (2 Thessalonians 2:9–12)

9. According to this passage, are people simply victims of Satan's deception, or are they also active participants/agents in the process? How so?

_____

_____

_____

_____

_____

_____

_____

He is proud.

> *The king will do as he pleases, exalting himself and claiming to be greater than every god there is, even blaspheming the God of gods. He will succeed—until the time of wrath is completed. For what has been determined will surely take place. He will have no regard for the gods of his ancestors, or for the god beloved of women, or for any other god, for he will boast that he is greater than them all.* (Daniel 11:36–37)

10. Why will the Antichrist blaspheme God? (Hint: see also Isaiah 14:12–14.)

_____

_____

_____

_____

_____

He is violent.

When they [the two witnesses of the Tribulation] complete their testimony, the beast that comes up out of the bottomless pit will declare war against them. He will conquer them and kill them. (Revelation 11:7)

And the beast was allowed to wage war against God's holy people and to overcome them. (Revelation 13:7)

"The Beast that John saw is the Antichrist—fast like a leopard, strong like a bear, and boastful like a lion roaring to assert its power. He comes out of the sea, which in this kind of setting refers to the Gentiles as opposed to the Jews, who come from the land of Israel.

"So the Beast will be a Gentile, possibly a European because Europe contains the remnants of the old Roman Empire and will be the center of a revived empire. The 'diadems' or crowns the Beast is wearing are ten nations over which he will rule."[1]

Tony Evans

---

11. How do twenty centuries of martyrdom (Christians being tortured, maimed, and killed for their faith) show you the true nature of the Evil One, who will eventually exercise as much destructiveness as he is allowed?

_____

_____

_____

_____

12. Given the way Satan operates, what can we assume about the kind of religious groups that urge their adherents to kill in the name of God?

_____

_____

_____

_____

Finding the Connection

Realizing in our heart of hearts that we have a brutal and vicious enemy who hates God (and thus everything and everyone associated with God) is sobering. Life is not a game. It is not a walk in the park. Everything is on the line.

Behind all the trivial and mundane activities of life, beneath the superficial façade of our entertainment culture lurks one with murderous intent. He is pure evil, a malevolent, cosmic terrorist. Though he is doomed to destruction and cannot ultimately win his battle against the Almighty, the devil (manifested in the end times by the Antichrist) intends to take as many souls with him as possible.

He will blind the minds of unbelievers (2 Corinthians 4:4), and he will attempt to distract and destroy believers using any and all means. Take note again of these sobering warnings from the pages of the New Testament:

Be on guard. Stand true to what you believe. Be courageous. Be strong. (1 Corinthians 16:13)

Pray at all times and on every occasion in the power of the Holy Spirit. Stay alert and be persistent in your prayers for all Christians everywhere. (Ephesians 6:18)

Devote yourselves to prayer with an alert mind and a thankful heart. (Colossians 4:2)

So be on your guard, not asleep like the others. Stay alert and be sober.
(1 Thessalonians 5:6)

With the help of the Holy Spirit who lives within us, carefully guard what has been entrusted to you. (2 Timothy 1:14)

13. What do these passages tell you about real life in this present age?

_____

_____

_____

_____

_____

_____

14. How does it make you feel to realize you are a target of the Evil One?

_____

_____

_____

_____

_____

_____

15. What tools has God given us to withstand the assault of evil?

_____

_____

_____

_____

_____

_____

POWERFUL . . . BUT NOT OMNIPOTENT!

"How much power does the devil have? Just as much as God allows him to have and not one whit more! Even as you read these words, Satan is a hapless player in the drama that he himself set in motion. And there is nothing he can do to change the outcome." [2]

Erwin Lutzer

Making the Change

(*Tribulation Force*, pp. 3–4)

Because of the saving and illuminating work of the Holy Spirit, a handful of folks at the beginning of the Left Behind series saw Nicolae for what he truly was.

BIZARRE AS IT MIGHT SEEM, Rayford Steele was one of only four people on the planet who knew the truth about Nicolae Carpathia—that he was a liar, a hypnotic brainwasher, the Antichrist himself. Others might suspect Carpathia of being other than he seemed, but only Rayford, his daughter, his pastor, and his new friend journalist Buck Williams knew for sure.

Buck had been one of the seventeen in that United Nations meeting room. And he had witnessed something entirely different—not a murder/suicide, but a double murder. Carpathia himself, according to Buck, had methodically borrowed the guard's gun, forced his old friend Jonathan Stonagal to kneel, then killed Stonagal and the British ambassador with one shot.

Carpathia had choreographed the murders, and then, while the witnesses sat in horror, Carpathia quietly told them what they had seen—the same story the newspapers now carried. Every witness in that room but one corroborated it. Most chilling, they believed it. Even Steve Plank, Buck's former boss, now Carpathia's press agent. Even Hattie Durham, Rayford's onetime flight attendant, who had become Carpathia's personal assistant. Everyone except Buck Williams.

Rayford had been dubious when Buck told his version in Bruce Barnes's office two nights ago. "You're the only person in the room who saw it your way?" he had challenged the writer.

"Captain Steele," Buck had said, "we all saw it the same way. But then Carpathia calmly described what he wanted us to think we had seen, and everybody but me immediately accepted it as truth. I want to know how he explains that he had the dead man's successor already there and sworn in when the murder took place. But now there's no evidence I was even there. It's as if Carpathia washed me from their memories. People I know now swear I wasn't there, and they aren't joking."

Chloe and Bruce Barnes had looked at each other and then back at Buck. Buck had finally become a believer, just before entering the meeting at the U.N. "I'm absolutely convinced that if I had gone into that room without God," Buck said, "I would have been reprogrammed too."

"But now if you just tell the world the truth—"

"Sir, I've been reassigned to Chicago because my boss believes I missed that meeting. Steve Plank asked why I had not accepted his invitation. I haven't talked to Hattie yet, but you know she won't remember I was there."

"The biggest question," Bruce Barnes said, "is what Carpathia thinks is in your head. Does he think he's erased the truth from your mind? If he knows you know, you're in grave danger."

16. What was the reason Buck was able to withstand the deceptive power of Nicolae?

_____

_____

_____

_____

_____

_____

17. Ephesians 1:13 (NIV) speaks of believers being "sealed . . . with the Holy Spirit." What does this mean for those of us who know Christ?

_____

_____

_____

_____

_____

"The concept of *sealing* includes the idea of ownership, authority and security. Since God has sealed us, we are his possession, secure (unless there were someone with greater power than God himself!) until the day of redemption. One of the best illustrations of sealing is registered mail. When something is registered at the post office, it is sealed until delivered, and only two persons can open it—the sender or the recipient. In our case, God is both sender and recipient, so only God could break that seal; and he has promised to deliver us to heaven. That's eternal security in the clearest terms."[3]

Charles Ryrie

18. Can you recall a time in your life when you understood your need for forgiveness—in short, for a real relationship with God? Have you trusted in Jesus' death on the cross and his free offer of pardon and life? If so, describe briefly how that came about.

_____

_____

_____

_____

_____

_____

19. If not, is there any reason you would not want to ask Christ to rescue you and transform you right now?

_____

_____

_____

_____

_____

Pursuing the Truth

Many Old Testament prophecies have *dual fulfillments;* that is, they refer to a near historical incident, but they also point to a distant future event or person in the distant future. A prime example of this is Isaiah 7:14. The ultimate future fulfillment of this prophecy was the miraculous birth of Christ to his mother, a virgin (see Luke 2). But many conservative scholars also believe this prophecy was intended to serve as a sign to King Ahaz, the ruler of Judah at the time Isaiah lived. In essence, God had Isaiah marry a young, chaste woman (an acceptable translation of the Hebrew word *virgin*). She would then give birth to a son, and before that child knew "right from wrong," both Assyria and the northern kingdom of Israel would be captured (Isaiah 7:16). When these detailed predictions actually transpired, Ahaz and the people of the southern kingdom would know that God was with them. Daniel 8:23–25 says:

> *At the end of their rule, when their sin is at its height, a fierce king, a master of intrigue, will rise to power. He will become very strong, but not by his own power. He will cause a*

shocking amount of destruction and succeed in everything he does. He will destroy power-
ful leaders and devastate the holy people. He will be a master of deception, defeating many
by catching them off guard. Without warning he will destroy them. He will even take on
the Prince of princes in battle, but he will be broken, though not by human power.

20. While speaking most immediately of the evil Syrian ruler and invader of Israel, Antiochus Epiphanes (175–164 B.C.), in what ways might this passage point also to the nature of the future Antichrist? What ominous qualities are listed here?

_____

_____

_____

_____

_____

_____

21. According to the following passage, what practical help is available as you try to understand the true nature of the enemy?

Be careful! Watch out for attacks from the Devil, your great enemy. He prowls around like
a roaring lion, looking for some victim to devour. Take a firm stand against him, and be
strong in your faith. Remember that Christians all over the world are going through the
same kind of suffering you are. (1 Peter 5:8–9)

_____

_____

_____

_____

_____

22. List as many specific ways as you can to "be strong in your faith." What does that look like in real, everyday terms?

_____

_____

_____

_____

_____

_____

_____

23. Think of two or three friends with whom you can share the results of this study. Write their names here. Pray for them and for an opportunity to speak with them.

_____

_____

_____

_____

_____

"Satan has always been a counterfeiter of spiritual realities, and in the Tribulation he hones his devilish art to a fine point. As God is a Trinity, so the devil tries to create his own kind of trinity: Satan in the role of the Father, Antichrist in the role of the Son, and of the false prophet in the role of the Holy Spirit. Just as the Holy Spirit does not call attention to himself but directs all worship to the Son, so the false prophet does not call attention to himself but directs all false worship to the Antichrist. The three members of this unholy trinity work together to accomplish their foul ends."[4]

Tim LaHaye and Jerry B. Jenkins

Lesson in Review . . .

- The Antichrist is "Satan incarnate" in the last days.
- Antichrist will come on the world scene during the Tribulation period.
- The nature of this beast is that he is powerful, deceitful, proud, and violent.
- The spirit of Antichrist is already here on the earth.
- Christians need to be sober and alert, realizing we are at war with the devil!

LEFT

BIBLE STUDY GUIDE #2

BEHIND

The Antichrist

Lesson 4
The Beast's Assistant

1. Think about famous sidekicks from TV, history, literature, and the movies; for example, Barney Fife (Andy Griffith's deputy) or Robin (Batman's partner). Which sidekick do you think is:

   the funniest?
   scariest?
   most helpful?
   most likable?
   the biggest bumbler?

   _____
   _____
   _____
   _____
   _____

2. If you could have anyone as your sidekick, who would you choose, and why?

   _____
   _____
   _____
   _____
   _____
   _____

3. If you could be the associate/assistant of any famous person or leader, who might that be? Why?

_____

_____

_____

_____

_____

Unfolding the Story

(*The Indwelling*, pp. 337, 347)

In *The Indwelling*, book seven of the Left Behind series, we read about the assassination of Nicolae Carpathia, former president of Romania, former secretary-general of the United Nations, and self-appointed Global Community potentate. Leon Fortunato, the world leader's second-in-command, eulogizes the dead leader before a massive throng gathered in person and watching on television:

> "**DESPAIRING OF OUR FUTURE,** regretting the past, we prayed in our own ways to our own gods for someone to take us by the hand and lead us through the minefields of our own making and into the blessedness of hope.
>
> "How could we have known that our prayers would be answered by one who would prove his own divinity over and over as he humbly, selflessly served, giving of himself even to the point of death to show us the way to healing? . . . .
>
> "I am pleased to report that the image you see to my left, your right, though larger than life, is an exact replica of Nicolae Carpathia, worthy of your reverence, yea, worthy of your worship.
>
> "Should you feel inclined to bow to the image after paying your respects, feel free. Bow, pray, sing, gesture—do whatever you wish to express your heart. And believe. Believe, people, that Nicolae Carpathia is indeed here in spirit and accepts your praise and worship. Many of you know that this so-called man, whom I know to be divine, personally raised me from the dead."

4. Close your eyes and imagine yourself at this bizarre end-times event. How do you think you'd feel?

_____

_____

_____

_____

_____

5. Compare Leon Fortunato to Nicolae Carpathia. How are the two leaders alike? How are they different?

_____

_____

_____

_____

_____

Back to Reality

Those of us who live in the West with freedom of religious expression have a hard time relating to such an experience. Being encouraged to bow down to another human and offer *worship?!* It sounds unbelievable. *No way would I ever do that,* we think.

Yet we *do* encounter regular (usually more subtle) pressure to please our superiors (or employers), to fit in with our peer groups, to avoid rocking the proverbial boat. You don't have to be at the funeral of the Antichrist in order to feel threatened to compromise your Christian convictions.

6. When and where have you been most tempted to deny your faith in Christ (or at least downplay its importance to you)? What happened? How did you feel?

_____

_____

_____

_____

_____

7. How do you respond when you hear stories about Christians in other countries resisting great persecution and being martyred for refusing to renounce their faith?

_____

_____

_____

_____

_____

_____

8. Do you think it's possible for a person to sell his/her soul to the devil? Why or why not?

_____

_____

_____

_____

_____

_____

Understanding the Word

In this study of the end times, we've looked at the dragon, Satan, and the Antichrist (who is "Satan incarnate" during the end times). But the Bible introduces another key character in this cosmic drama. Together these three will comprise an unholy trinity in the last days. Theirs is an evil attempt to imitate the triune God.

Consider this shocking, revealing passage from Revelation 13:

I saw another beast come up out of the earth. He had two horns like those of a lamb, and he spoke with the voice of a dragon. He exercised all the authority of the first beast. And he required all the earth and those who belong to this world to worship the first beast, whose death-wound had been healed. He did astounding miracles, such as making fire flash down to earth from heaven while everyone was watching. And with all the miracles he was allowed to perform on behalf of the first beast, he deceived all the people who belong to this world. He ordered the people of the world to make a great statue of the first beast, who was fatally wounded and then came back to life. He was permitted to give life to this statue so that it could speak. Then the statue commanded that anyone refusing to worship it must die.

He required everyone—great and small, rich and poor, slave and free—to be given a mark on the right hand or on the forehead. And no one could buy or sell anything without that mark, which was either the name of the beast or the number representing his name. Wisdom is needed to understand this. Let the one who has understanding solve the number of the beast, for it is the number of a man. His number is 666. (Revelation 13:11–18)

9. What is the job description of this "second beast"? (Jot down the various phrases used by the apostle John to describe the character and activity of this person, who theologians often refer to as "the false prophet.")

_____

_____

_____

_____

_____

_____

"Another beast? Who is this character?"

"This man is Antichrist's lieutenant, who will enforce the worship of Antichrist by performing miracles (Revelation 13:13), by making and animating an image of Antichrist (13:14–15), by sentencing to death those who disobey (13:15), and by requiring a mark on the hand or forehead in order that men may buy and sell (13:16–17)."[1]

Charles Ryrie

10. What are we to make of the false prophet's miracle-working power? How should this alter the way we interpret seemingly "miraculous" events and claims?

_____

_____

_____

_____

_____

_____

11. What do you think it means that the false prophet gives life to the statue of the Antichrist? What are some ways in which modern technology is already able to make inanimate things seem alive?

_____

_____

_____

_____

_____

"Most commentators believe he [the false prophet] is of Jewish descent, since John says he comes up 'out of the earth' (Palestine) rather than out of the 'sea' (the Gentile world) as does the Beast. That he has two horns 'like a lamb' suggests he will try to appear as gentle as 'the Lamb of God,' but this is nothing but a sham, for he speaks 'like a dragon,' eager to declare the very words of the devil.

"The false prophet will be the Antichrist's primary minister of propaganda, just as Goebbels was for Hitler. Unlike Goebbels, however, the false prophet will have the power to do 'great signs' while in the presence of the Antichrist, even calling down fire from heaven—just as the two witnesses of Revelation 11 are said to do. In this way he will deceive the unregenerate masses of the earth to worship the Beast." [2]

Tim LaHaye and Jerry B. Jenkins

Finding the Connection

One of the themes in the Left Behind books, and the bottom-line issue in our own lives, is the theme of genuine worship. What, exactly, is worship? Our English word _worship_ is derived from the Old English word _worthship,_ meaning "the state of having worth." In other words, worship is about what we value most. The question isn't, "_Will_ people worship?"—everyone on earth values something or someone above all else. The question is, "_Who_ or _what_ will we worship?"

Whatever we give our attention to, whatever we regard as worthy of our time and energy and best efforts, that is—in a practical sense—what we worship.

Where is _your_ attention, affection, and adoration directed? Toward the accumulation of money? Toward impressing others? To exercising power? Children, homes, careers, hobbies, sensual experiences/pleasures, desires for prestige or significance—all of these can become gods—idols—in our lives if they dominate our thinking, our choices, our desires.

The great theologian Augustine wisely observed, "You have made us for yourself, O God, and our hearts are restless until they find rest in you." Until God owns our hearts, until he fills our minds, until he alone is the consuming passion of our souls, we will scramble about in frustration, seeking something to give our lives to. He only is worthy of all that we are and have. Nothing and no one else in the universe deserves maximum honor and glory and praise.

12. How passionate are you about acknowledging the worth of God? Could people look at your personal calendar and your checkbook and get an immediate sense that God is foremost in your life?

_____

_____

_____

_____

_____

13. An idol isn't merely a carved statue or totem pole. Idolatry isn't just a practice among pagans in primitive cultures. An idol is anything that takes the place of God in our lives. When anything or anyone other than God is preeminent in our thoughts or uppermost in our affections, we are guilty of idolatry. What about you? What rivals for God do you see in your life?

_____

_____

_____

_____

_____

Consider the white-hot, heavenly worship that John was allowed to glimpse:

> Then I looked again, and I heard the singing of thousands and millions of angels around the throne and the living beings and the elders. And they sang in a mighty chorus:
> "The Lamb is worthy—the Lamb who was killed. He is worthy to receive power and riches and wisdom and strength and honor and glory and blessing."

And then I heard every creature in heaven and on earth and in the sea. They also sang: "Blessing and honor and glory and power belong to the one sitting on the throne and to the Lamb forever and ever."

And the four living beings said, "Amen!" And the twenty-four elders fell down and worshiped God and the Lamb. (Revelation 5:11–14)

14. How does this scene compare to your own habits of worship? to your church services?

_____

_____

_____

_____

_____

15. Why are so many Christians so passionless in their worship? Why do many get more excited at sports events than in worship of the living God?

_____

_____

_____

_____

_____

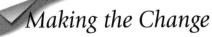

Making the Change

(*The Indwelling*, pp. 348–49)

Right now Christians in the West can (mostly) worship freely. We generally do not have to fear severe reprisals for being followers of Jesus. Our brothers and sisters living in atheistic nations and areas dominated by radical Islam or militant Hinduism are not so fortunate. They could probably relate well to the rest of the message given by Leon Fortunato at Nicolae Carpathia's funeral:

> "TODAY," FORTUNATO INTONED, "I am instituting a new, improved global faith that shall have as its object of worship this image, which represents the very spirit of Nicolae Carpathia. Listen carefully, my people. When I said a moment ago that you may worship this image and Nicolae himself if you felt so inclined, I was merely being

polite. Silence, please. With global citizenship comes responsibility, and that responsibility entails subordination to those in authority over you. . . .

"As your new ruler, it is only fair of me to tell you that there is no option as it pertains to worshiping the image and spirit of Nicolae Carpathia. He is not only part of our new religion, but he is also its centerpiece. Indeed, he has become and forever shall be our religion. Now before you . . . bow before the image, let me impress upon your mind the consequences of disobeying such an edict."

Suddenly, from the statue itself—with its great expanses of black smoke now nearly blotting out the sun—came a thundering pronouncement: "I am the lord your god who sits high above the heavens! . . . I am the god above all other gods. There is none like me. Worship or beware!"

Fortunato suddenly spoke softly, fatherly. "Fear not," he said. "Lift your eyes to the heavens." The massive dark clouds dissipated, and the image appeared serene once more. "Nicolae Carpathia loves you and has only your best in mind. Charged with the responsibility of ensuring compliance with the worship of your god, I have also been imbued with power. Please stand. . . .

"Let us assume that there may be those here who choose, for one reason or another, to refuse to worship Carpathia. Perhaps they are independent spirits. Perhaps they are rebellious Jews. Perhaps they are secret Judah-ites who still believe 'their man' is the only way to God. Regardless of their justification, they shall surely die."

Remember, this imaginative series *is* based on biblical prophecy. Antichrist *will* rise to power. He *will* suffer a fatal head wound (Revelation 13:3, 14) and then come back to life. At his side the false prophet *will* serve, presiding over a one-world religion, administering the mark of the beast (see the next lesson), and demanding the inhabitants of earth in the end times to worship the beast.

"The job of this Satan-inspired creature will be to mimic the Holy Spirit's relationship to Christ. The Holy Spirit's role is to bring praise and worship to Christ, so the False Prophet's assignment will be to bring praise and worship to the false Christ, the Antichrist."[3]

Tony Evans

16. How do these events remind you of the story of Shadrach, Meshach, and Abednego found in Daniel 3?

_____

_____

_____

_____

_____

17. How devoted are *you* to Christ? Could your faith endure a severe test? Does it worry you sometimes that under extreme pressure you might renounce your allegiance to Jesus?

_____

_____

_____

_____

_____

If you have compromised your convictions and been unfaithful to Christ in some way, then the metamorphosis in Peter's life will give you hope. After Jesus was arrested, Peter denied Christ:

> *A servant girl noticed him in the firelight and began staring at him. Finally she said, "This man was one of Jesus' followers!" Peter denied it. "Woman," he said, "I don't even know the man!"* (Luke 22:56–57)

A few weeks later, following Christ's resurrection and a gracious beachside encounter with the One he had denied, Peter is an altogether different disciple. Later, when hauled in with John before the powerful Jewish ruling body, a Spirit-filled Peter preaches a rousing message:

> *"Leaders and elders of our nation . . . Jesus is the one referred to in the Scriptures, where it says, 'The stone that you builders rejected has now become the cornerstone.' There is salvation in no one else! There is no other name in all of heaven for people to call on to save them."*
>
> *The members of the council were amazed when they saw the boldness of Peter and John, for they could see that they were ordinary men who had had no special training. They also recognized them as men who had been with Jesus. . . . "Perhaps we can stop them from spreading their propaganda. We'll warn them not to speak to anyone in Jesus' name again." So they . . . told them never again to speak or teach about Jesus.*

But Peter and John replied, "Do you think God wants us to obey you rather than him? We cannot stop telling about the wonderful things we have seen and heard." (Acts 4:8, 11–13, 17–20)

18. How do you account for Peter's stunning change? What hope does this give you?

_____

_____

_____

_____

_____

_____

Pursuing the Truth

19. Read Revelation 16:13–14 below. What does this passage suggest about the way the dragon, the beast, and the false prophet work together?

And I saw three evil spirits that looked like frogs leap from the mouth of the dragon, the beast, and the false prophet. These miracle-working demons caused all the rulers of the world to gather for battle against the Lord on that great judgment day of God Almighty.

_____

_____

_____

_____

"For three and a half short years the false prophet will force the unredeemed multitudes to worship the Antichrist; for eternity he will be punished. For three and a half short years he will seek to usurp Christ's glory; for endless ages he will be excluded from that glory. For three and a half short years he will wage war against the saints and take away their earthly lives; for an infinity of years he will suffer destruction and the agonies of the second death. Not a very good trade, is it?"[4]

Tim LaHaye and Jerry B. Jenkins

20. We touched on this earlier, but it is worth revisiting. If we witness an event that seems to be miraculous, can we automatically conclude God is behind it? Why or why not?

_____

_____

_____

_____

_____

_____

21. What truth or fact or principle from this lesson hits you the hardest? Why?

_____

_____

_____

_____

_____

22. What's been the most encouraging passage you've read in the Left Behind series? the most troubling?

_____

_____

_____

_____

_____

Lesson in Review . . .

- The false prophet or "second beast" of Revelation 13 is the third member of the unholy trinity that will dominate the earth during the Tribulation.
- Just as the Holy Spirit seeks to bring glory to Christ, the false prophet will seek to get people to honor and obey the Antichrist.
- This false prophet will use deception, miraculous power, and murderous threats to enforce worship of the beast.

LEFT

BEHIND

The Antichrist

Lesson 5
The Résumé of the Beast

1. What is the most impressive feature on your résumé?

2. What are some of your greatest achievements? How would you like to be remembered by your family and friends?

> "Knowing what the Bible says about this future Antichrist can give us *hope*. Even as we watch the world seeming to slide toward the end times, we are reminded that God is in control and that his program for the church ends before his final seven-year program for Israel resumes. Today's headlines simply mean that our redemption is nearer today than it has ever been, . . . and that gives us hope."[1]
>
> Charles H. Dyer

Unfolding the Story

(*The Mark*, pp. 83–87)

The eighth book in the Left Behind series is *The Mark*, which depicts the resurrected Antichrist, Nicolae Carpathia, ruling the planet with an iron fist. His goal is nothing less than to be worshiped by all, and his plan is diabolical:

> "THE FIRST PAGE OF YOUR FOLDERS . . . is a listing of the ten world regions and a corresponding number. It is the product of a mathematical equation that identifies those regions and their relationships to His Excellency the Potentate. The loyalty mark, which I shall explain in detail, shall begin with these numbers, thus identifying the home region of every citizen. The subsequent numbers, embedded on a biochip inserted under the skin, will further identify the person to the point where every one shall be unique."
>
> Suddenly, as if in a trance, Leon rose and began to speak. "Every man, woman, and child, regardless of their station in life, shall receive this mark on their right hands or on their foreheads. Those who neglect to get the mark when it is made available will not be allowed to buy or sell until such time as they receive it. Those who overtly refuse it shall be put to death, and every marked loyal citizen shall be deputized with the right and the responsibility to report such a one. The mark shall consist of the name of His Excellency or the prescribed number.". . .
>
> "The beauty of the embedded chip is twofold. . . . First it leaves the visible evidence of loyalty to the potentate, and second, it serves as a method of payment and receipting for buying and selling. Eye-level scanners will allow customers and merchants to merely pass by and be billed or receipted."

3. Sitting in this briefing was David Hassid, a secret believer in Jesus. What do you suppose he was thinking as he heard this news?

_____

_____

_____

_____

_____

_____

4. Also part of Nicolae's ruthless plan was the use of guillotines for those who resisted the mark. How effective is the threat of torture and death in getting people to comply? What kind of leaders and nations resort to this tactic?

_____

_____

_____

_____

Back to Reality

Some readers have expressed disbelief at this plot twist in the Left Behind series. "Some kind of number imbedded in our foreheads or hands?! That's preposterous—that could never happen!" they argue. But think about our everyday life right now. Retina scanning technology, the growing number of businesses (even fast-food restaurants!) that take credit cards, advances in microchip technology, birth-control medication that is imbedded under the skin.

5. How, if at all, could these developments lead to the kind of situation described in the excerpt on the previous page (and in the Bible)?

_____

_____

_____

_____

"People . . . used to wonder how the Antichrist would ever be able to imprint the number 666 on people so that he could wield absolute economic control.

"But with the advent of computer microchips and the other technology we are seeing emerge today, that question doesn't come up as much. A technological context is being created in which the right person at the right time could not only control the economies of entire nations, but track the whereabouts of each person in a nation twenty-four hours a day."[2]

Tony Evans

6. Someone has restated the Golden Rule this way: "He who has the gold makes the rules." In what way does economic control lead to power? Why do some people insist that the head of the Federal Reserve Bank is, perhaps, the most powerful man on earth?

    _____

    _____

    _____

7. Someone else has observed: "Power corrupts. Absolute power corrupts absolutely." What is it about gaining more and more control that fosters a growing evil? Where have you seen examples of this in the world or in your life?

    _____

    _____

    _____

    _____

A KEY TO UNDERSTANDING BIBLICAL PROPHECY: CORRECTLY INTERPRET DANIEL 9:24–27

The angel Gabriel delivered this prophecy to Daniel in about 538 B.C. while the people of God are in Babylonian captivity:

> A period of seventy sets of seven has been decreed for your people and your holy city to put down rebellion, to bring an end to sin, to atone for guilt, to bring in everlasting righteousness, to confirm the prophetic vision, and to anoint the Most Holy Place. Now listen and understand! Seven sets of seven plus sixty-two sets of seven will pass from the time the command is given to rebuild Jerusalem until the Anointed One comes. Jerusalem will be rebuilt with streets and strong defenses, despite the perilous times.
>
> After this period of sixty-two sets of seven, the Anointed One will be killed, appearing to have accomplished nothing, and a ruler will arise whose armies will destroy the city and the Temple. The end will come with a flood, and war and its miseries are decreed from that time to the very end. He will make a treaty with the people for a period of one set of seven, but after half this time, he will put an end to the sacrifices and offerings. Then as a climax to all his terrible deeds, he will set up a sacrilegious object that causes desecration, until the end that has been decreed is poured out on this defiler. (Daniel 9:24–27)

This cryptic paragraph, known to Bible scholars and theologians as "Daniel's prophecy of the seventy weeks," is a key paragraph in understanding things to come. Nevertheless, it has long confused Christians. The following chart is a concise explanation of what Daniel's prediction says and means:

The phrase "seventy sets of seven" (v. 24) refers to seventy sets of seven *years* (note the context—9:2—where Daniel had been reading in *Jeremiah* about the seventy *years* of captivity).

Simple multiplication tells us that "seventy sets of seven *years*" = 490 years.

The angel Gabriel listed six things (v. 24) that would happen during this 490-year period:

1. "put down rebellion" = Israel would be brought to repentance

2. "bring an end to sin" = Israel would be granted spiritual life through the new covenant

3. "atone for guilt" = Christ would die for sin

4. "bring in everlasting righteousness" = Christ would establish his kingdom

5. "confirm the prophetic vision" = fulfillment of all prophecies related to Israel

6. "anoint the Most Holy Place" = perhaps a reference to the millennial temple

Verse 25 clearly states that sixty-nine sets ("seven sets . . . plus sixty-two sets") of seven years, or 483 years total, would pass from the time the command was given to rebuild Jerusalem until the killing of Messiah.

The Persian king Artaxerxes gave the command to rebuild Jerusalem in 444 B.C. (see Nehemiah 2:1).

Calculating with 30-day months and 360-day prophetic years (a standard practice, see Genesis 7:11, 24; 8:4; Numbers 20:29; Deuteronomy 34:8), we determine that 483 years = 173,880 days.

Count forward that many days from 444 B.C. and you come to March A.D. 33, the very month in which Jesus was crucified (v. 26)!

The first sixty-nine sets of seven years are thus historical. They have already happened.

However, when Jesus the Messiah was rejected and killed by his own people, *the prophetic clock stopped;* God put Israel in a kind of national and prophetic "time-out."

Then God unveiled a previously unknown part of his eternal plan—the entity we know as the church.

We are in the church age now, but God has not forgotten his promises to Israel.

There is still one last set of seven years (the seventieth set of seven years) to go!

That final set of seven years is the future period known as the Tribulation.

According to Daniel's prophecy, the Antichrist will begin this final seven-year period by making a treaty with Israel (v. 27).

He will then break the peace treaty after three and a half years.

The final half of this last seven-year period (forty-two months—see Revelation 11:2; 13:5; or 1,260 days—see Revelation 11:3; 12:6) is the terrible time of judgment we know as the Great Tribulation.

When Daniel's ancient prophecy is laid next to the visions John received on Patmos (the book we know as Revelation), and when we also add the other New Testament teaching on the end times, the mysterious puzzle of the last days begins to comes together. God doesn't want his people to be in the dark!

8. Carefully read through the list of prophetic events above. Mark any that you find curious or difficult to understand. What two or three questions come to mind as you review the list? Jot them below and keep them for further study. You may discover answers as we proceed.

_____

_____

_____

_____

_____

_____

Understanding the Word

When we piece together the various prophecies pertaining to the Antichrist's activities in the last days, we come up with a résumé that includes the following highlights.

He rises to power as a peacemaker.

> He will make a treaty with the people for a period of one set of seven, but after half this time, he will put an end to the sacrifices and offerings. Then as a climax to all his terrible deeds, he will set up a sacrilegious object that causes desecration, until the end that has been decreed is poured out on this defiler. (Daniel 9:27)

9. Today, a Muslim mosque (the Dome of the Rock in Jerusalem) sits on the site where the Jews want to rebuild their temple and reinstitute their sacrificial system. The Antichrist

will somehow have a plan to resolve this ancient dispute. Because of his diplomacy, the Jews and Arabs will enter into a "deal" to live together peacefully. How do you think that might work?

_____

_____

_____

_____

_____

"Our world today is longing for peace. Imagine how the world would embrace a leader who could step up and settle the age-old conflict in the Middle East with one stroke of brilliant diplomacy. Imagine how people would welcome someone who could give them economic stability in return for a little more control over their lives. History proves that people will surrender their rights for stability and a sense of peace in times of chaos.

"The Antichrist will be able to deliver peace and stability, and the unbelieving world will welcome him as he spends the first three and a half years of the Tribulation solidifying his power and gaining control.

"This leader will be able to bring all peoples together and appear to be able to end racial conflict, ethnic cleansing, class destruction, and religious tension. The conditions are ripe for the emergence of such a dictator."[3]

Tony Evans

He kills those who oppose him.

And I will give power to my two witnesses, and they will be clothed in sackcloth and will prophesy during those 1,260 days.

These two prophets are the two olive trees and the two lampstands that stand before the Lord of all the earth. If anyone tries to harm them, fire flashes from the mouths of the prophets and consumes their enemies. This is how anyone who tries to harm them must die. They have power to shut the skies so that no rain will fall for as long as they prophesy. And they have the power to turn the rivers and oceans into blood, and to send every kind of plague upon the earth as often as they wish.

When they complete their testimony, the beast that comes up out of the bottomless pit will declare war against them. He will conquer them and kill them. And their bodies will lie in the main street of Jerusalem, the city which is called "Sodom" and "Egypt," the city where their Lord was crucified. And for three and a half days, all peoples, tribes, languages, and nations will come to stare at their bodies. No one will be allowed to bury them. All the people who belong to this world will give presents to each other to celebrate the death of the two prophets who had tormented them.

But after three and a half days, the spirit of life from God entered them, and they stood up! And terror struck all who were staring at them. Then a loud voice shouted from heaven, "Come up here!" And they rose to heaven in a cloud as their enemies watched. (Revelation 11:3–12)

10. The two witnesses of Revelation 11 will be a thorn in the side of Antichrist. Preaching the truth nonstop, they will finally enrage the beast and will pay for it with their lives. But according to the Bible, what will happen then?

_____

_____

_____

_____

He seeks the worship of all.

I saw another beast come up out of the earth. He had two horns like those of a lamb, and he spoke with the voice of a dragon. He exercised all the authority of the first beast. And he required all the earth and those who belong to this world to worship the first beast, whose death-wound had been healed. He did astounding miracles, such as making fire flash down to earth from heaven while everyone was watching. And with all the miracles he was allowed to perform on behalf of the first beast, he deceived all the people who belong to this world. He ordered the people of the world to make a great statue of the first beast, who was fatally wounded and then came back to life. He was permitted to give life to this statue so that it could speak. Then the statue commanded that anyone refusing to worship it must die. (Revelation 13:11–15)

11. What are we to make of the beast's fatal head wound and his "resurrection"? What is this intended to counterfeit?

_____

_____

_____

_____

He uses financial coercion to gain widespread loyalty.

> *He required everyone—great and small, rich and poor, slave and free—to be given a mark on the right hand or on the forehead. And no one could buy or sell anything without that mark, which was either the name of the beast or the number representing his name. Wisdom is needed to understand this. Let the one who has understanding solve the number of the beast, for it is the number of a man. His number is 666.* (Revelation 13:16–18)

12. The false prophet will, with the full approval of the beast, preside over a worldwide system of commerce. Describe that coming system. How will it work?

_____

_____

_____

_____

_____

> "A 'mark' is an impression made by a stamp, such as a brand used on slaves and animals. Men will become slaves to the man of sin and will have to bear the identifying mark of their slavery. Perhaps timid slaves will have the mark placed in their right hands. To avoid embarrassment, they may try to avoid shaking hands with people in order to conceal the mark. Bold followers of Antichrist may have the mark placed in the middle of their foreheads.
>
> "What will this mark be like? . . . It will be either the name of the beast or his number, and the number is further explained as 666. . . . This number has been linked to so many personages as to make them all unreliable coincidences. When this great ruler comes to power, however, there will be no mistake as to who he is. In some way unknown to us know, the number 666 will play a principal part in his identification."[4]
>
> Charles Ryrie

Finding the Connection

We use many expressions to describe the tough, pivotal moments in life: "No time for the squeamish." "Separating the men from the boys." "Crunch time."

Certainly, no moments are bigger than the future ones described in the Left Behind series. Those living in the Tribulation will face a monumental—make that, an *eternal*—

decision. *Everything* will be at stake. Will they choose a deceptive short-term "safety" or real long-term security?

And yet the choices *we* make *now* in our daily lives are also significant. Someone has said: "Sow a thought, reap an act; sow an act, reap a habit; sow a habit, reap a character; sow a character, reap a destiny."

Someone else has observed, "We make our choices, and then our choices make us."

Think about the choices you are making in these areas of your life:
- Marital
- Parental
- Educational
- Recreational
- Social
- Moral/ethical
- Occupational

13. On a scale of 1–10, with 1 being "evil" and 10 being "godly," how would you rate your decisions and actions in each of those areas over the last month? Take a few moments and, after reflection, write a number next to each of the areas above.

_____

_____

_____

14. Without trying to be morbid, if you were to die today, how would you be remembered? Which of the "grades" above would you rather not have on your permanent record?

_____

_____

_____

_____

_____

_____

_____

_____

15. We've seen the résumé of the Antichrist in this lesson. What is your résumé so far? In what ways would you like to change the course of your life?

_____

_____

_____

_____

_____

_____

_____

16. Why is the linking of money (or any "treasure") to the central pursuit of life such a dangerous thing? (Hint: see Matthew 6:19–24.)

_____

_____

_____

_____

17. What light does Jesus shed in Matthew 6:19–24 on the importance of what we choose to worship?

_____

_____

_____

Making the Change

(*The Mark*, pp. 337–39)

Tsion Ben-Judah is a key figure in the Left Behind books. A former Jewish scholar and statesman, Tsion came to believe that Jesus is the promised Messiah. After he revealed his newfound faith on international TV, his family was murdered. Tsion escaped to the United States and went into hiding, where he began cybercasting biblical truth to more than a billion people daily.

At the end of *The Mark,* Tsion sent out this communique:

"**I HAVE GATHERED FROM MANY** that one of your loftiest goals is to survive until the Glorious Appearing. I share that longing but wish to gently remind you that that is not our all in all. The apostle Paul said that to live is Christ but that to die is gain. While it would be thrilling beyond words to see the triumphant Lord Christ return to earth and set up his thousand-year reign, I believe I could learn to deal with it if I were called to heaven in advance and saw from that perspective instead.

"Beloved, our top priority now is not even thwarting the evils of Antichrist, though I engage in that effort every day. I want to confound him, revile him, enrage him, frustrate him, and get in the way of his plans every way I know how. His primary goal is ascendancy for himself, worship of himself, and the death and destruction of any who might otherwise become tribulation saints.

"So, as worthy and noble a goal as it is to go on the offensive against the evil one, I believe we can do that most effectively by focusing on persuading the undecided to come to faith. Knowing that every day could be our last, that we could be found out and dragged to a mark application center, there to make our decision to die for the sake of Christ, we must be more urgent about our task than ever.

"Many have written in fear, confessing that they do not believe they have the courage or the character to choose death over life when threatened with the guillotine. As a fellow pilgrim in this journey of faith, let me admit that I do not understand this either. In my flesh I am weak. I want to live. I am afraid of death, but even more of dying. The very thought of having my head severed from my body repulses me as much as it does anyone. In my worst nightmare I see myself standing before the GC operatives a weakling, a quivering mass who can do nothing but plead for his life. I envision myself breaking God's heart by denying my Lord. Oh, what an awful picture!

"In my most hated imagination I fail at the hour of testing and accept the mark of loyalty that we all know is the cursed mark of the beast, all because I so cherish my own life.

"Is that your fear today, friend? Are you all right as long as you are in hiding and somehow able to survive? But have you a foreboding about that day when you will be forced to publicly declare your faith or deny your Savior?

"I have good news for you that I have already admitted is difficult to understand, even for me, who has been called to shepherd you and exposit the Word of God for you. The Bible tells us that once one is either sealed by God as a believer or accepts the mark of loyalty to Antichrist, this is a once-and-for-all choice. In other words, if you have decided for Christ and the seal of God is evident on your forehead, you cannot change your mind.

"This tells me that somehow, when we face the ultimate test, God miraculously overcomes our evil, selfish flesh and gives us the grace and courage to make the right decision in spite of ourselves. My interpretation of this is that we will be unable to deny Jesus, unable to even choose the mark that would temporarily save our lives."

18. In the novel, how would this Internet message have affected its readers?

_____

_____

_____

_____

_____

19. Do you ever privately wonder about your own loyalty and commitment to Christ? Do you think you could stand up to extreme pressure to downplay or even renounce your faith? Why or why not?

_____

_____

_____

_____

_____

20. How can one know for *sure* that he or she is a true child of God? (Hint: see 1 John 5:11–13.) How would you describe *your* sense of certainty?

_____

_____

_____

_____

_____

"God has always intended prophecy to have a practical application to the here and now. So what? What difference does this truth make in our lives? . . . [K]nowing what the Bible says about this future leader should give us confidence that God is in control. God may end your life on earth and take you to heaven, but you can be sure that you will never die and go there by accident. You will pass from this life into eternity only when God decides that the time has come. He is in control."[5]

Charles H. Dyer

Pursuing the Truth

As those who are living in the generation that may very well see the events described in the Left Behind series, we need an eternal perspective. By keeping our eyes on the future, we live more effectively in the present. In fact, those who are most genuinely heavenly minded are the ones who do the most earthly good! Read the following counsel from God's Word:

> *Let heaven fill your thoughts. Do not think only about things down here on earth.* (Colossians 3:2)

21. To what degree is this your normal mind-set? In what ways do you desire to see an improvement in your heavenly mind-set?

_____

_____

_____

_____

_____

_____

Consider the following passage written by the apostle Paul to the Christians living in the corrupt city of Corinth:

> *Yes, we live under constant danger of death because we serve Jesus, so that the life of Jesus will be obvious in our dying bodies. So we live in the face of death, but it has resulted in eternal life for you.*

But we continue to preach because we have the same kind of faith the psalmist had when he said, "I believed in God, and so I speak." We know that the same God who raised our Lord Jesus will also raise us with Jesus and present us to himself along with you. All of these things are for your benefit. And as God's grace brings more and more people to Christ, there will be great thanksgiving, and God will receive more and more glory.

That is why we never give up. Though our bodies are dying, our spirits are being renewed every day. For our present troubles are quite small and won't last very long. Yet they produce for us an immeasurably great glory that will last forever! So we don't look at the troubles we can see right now; rather, we look forward to what we have not yet seen. For the troubles we see will soon be over, but the joys to come will last forever.
(2 Corinthians 4:11–18)

22. What was Paul's secret for enduring hard times?

_____

_____

_____

_____

_____

23. How did Paul compare his present life with the life awaiting him in eternity?

_____

_____

_____

_____

_____

24. As you assimilate these prophetic lessons into your daily living, what concerns, challenges, and desires do you want to keep praying about as you seek to live for God in these uncertain times?

_____

_____

_____

_____

25. List two people you'd like to share this information with. Ask one or two other Christians to pray with and for you as you approach these people with the gospel.

_____

_____

_____

_____

"Why must there be such a time as this [the Tribulation]? There are at least two reasons: First, the wickedness of man must be punished. God may seem to be doing nothing about evil now, but someday he will act. A second reason is that man must, by one means or another, be prostrated before the King of kings and Lord of lords. He may do so voluntarily now by coming to Christ in faith and receiving salvation. Later he will have to do so, receiving only condemnation."[6]

Charles Ryrie

Lesson in Review. . .

- Following the Rapture of the church, the Antichrist will catapult to power.
- He will sign a peace treaty with Israel—an event that will mark the beginning of Daniel's "seventieth set of seven" (the seven-year period known as the Tribulation).
- The Antichrist will kill God's witnesses and seek the worship of all living creatures.
- He will attempt to force the inhabitants of earth to worship him by controlling the world's economic system. Charles Ryrie sums up this program as "Bow or starve."

The Antichrist

Lesson 6
Damned! The Destiny of the Beast

1. Most fairy tales end with the sentence: "And they lived happily ever after." Is this *ever* the case in real life? What's your favorite all-time "ending" (i.e., in a book, movie, fairy tale, etc.)?

    _____

    _____

    _____

    _____

2. Are you one of those people who likes surprise endings, or do you go ahead and read the last chapter of a suspense novel so that you'll know how everything turns out?

    _____

    _____

    _____

    _____

Unfolding the Story
(*Desecration*, pp. 47, 100–101, 103)

Early in *Desecration*, the ninth book of the Left Behind series, Buck Williams and Chaim Rosenzweig are hiding at a big public rally honoring Nicolae Carpathia. They know he is the Antichrist and their goal is to disrupt the proceedings, warning as many people as possible of his true nature. The crowd begins singing the official song of praise to this satanic leader:

> **"HAIL CARPATHIA,** our lord and risen king;
> Hail Carpathia, rules o'er everything,
> We'll worship him until we die;
> He's our beloved Nicolae.
> Hail Carpathia, our lord and risen king."

Buck felt conspicuous not singing, but Chaim seemed not to care what anyone thought. He merely bowed his head and stared at the ground. When Leon [Fortunato, the false prophet] urged the people to "sing it once more as we welcome the object of our worship," people clapped and waved as they sang. Buck, ever the wordsmith, changed the lyrics on the spot and sang:

> "Fail, Carpathia, you fake and stupid thing;
> Fail, Carpathia, fool of everything.
> I'll hassle you until you die;
> You're headed for the lake of fire.
> Fail, Carpathia, you fake and stupid thing."

A short time later, Dr. Tsion Ben-Judah prepares to send the following message to his Internet flock of millions:

> **"TO MY DEAR TRIBULATION SAINTS,** believers in Jesus the Christ, the Messiah and our Lord and Savior, and to the curious, the undecided, and the enemies of our faith:
>
> "It has now become clear that Nicolae Carpathia, the one who calls himself the ruler of this world and whom I have identified (with the authority of the Holy Scriptures) as Antichrist, along with his False Prophet Leon Fortunato (upon whom has been bestowed the audacious title of the Most High Reverend Father of Carpathianism), has scheduled what the Bible calls the desecration of the temple. . . .
>
> "Antichrist has already begun fulfilling the prophecy that 'he shall go out with great fury to destroy and annihilate many.' Fortunately, someday 'he shall come to his end, and no one will help him.'. . .
>
> "Our hope is in the promise that 'the lawless one will be revealed, whom the Lord will consume with the breath of his mouth and destroy with the brightness of his coming.' "

3. Where did Buck say Nicolae Carpathia was headed?

_____

_____

4. What did Tsion say to sharpen the picture of the future of the Antichrist?

_____

_____

Back to Reality

No sane person would choose to live through the Tribulation and eagerly face the terrors we read about in the Bible and in the Left Behind series. However, even in a pre-Tribulation world right now, we have an ample supply of chaos and craziness and confusion.

5. How does an eternal perspective give us peace and confidence in these times?

_____

_____

_____

6. Why is it a good idea to keep in mind how this world will end and how God will finally and completely deal with evil—even if he doesn't do it in our lifetime?

_____

_____

_____

7. What, in your opinion, is wrong with the following (very common) reasoning?
   A. A good, loving, all-powerful God would bring an end to evil and suffering.
   B. But evil and suffering are rampant in the world (and getting worse).
   C. Therefore, God—if he exists at all—must not be good and/or loving and/or all-powerful.

_____

_____

Understanding the Word

Here's the good news—God has not left us to wonder how this great cosmic play called "life" is going to turn out. We do not have to wait anxiously until the end to see *if* the "bad guys" will get what's coming to them or *how* their complete defeat will come about. The last book in the Bible spells it all out quite clearly:

> *Then I saw heaven opened, and a white horse was standing there. And the one sitting on the horse was named Faithful and True. For he judges fairly and then goes to war. His eyes were bright like flames of fire, and on his head were many crowns. A name was written on him, and only he knew what it meant. He was clothed with a robe dipped in blood, and his title was the Word of God. The armies of heaven, dressed in pure white linen, followed him on white horses. From his mouth came a sharp sword, and with it he struck down the nations. He ruled them with an iron rod, and he trod the winepress of the fierce wrath of almighty God. On his robe and thigh was written this title: King of kings and Lord of lords.*
>
> *Then I saw an angel standing in the sun, shouting to the vultures flying high in the sky: "Come! Gather together for the great banquet God has prepared. Come and eat the flesh of kings, captains, and strong warriors; of horses and their riders; and of all humanity, both free and slave, small and great."*
>
> *Then I saw the beast gathering the kings of the earth and their armies in order to fight against the one sitting on the horse and his army. And the beast was captured, and with him the false prophet who did mighty miracles on behalf of the beast—miracles that deceived all who had accepted the mark of the beast and who worshiped his statue. Both the beast and his false prophet were thrown alive into the lake of fire that burns with sulfur. Their entire army was killed by the sharp sword that came out of the mouth of the one riding the white horse. And all the vultures of the sky gorged themselves on the dead bodies.* (Revelation 19:11–21)

8. How is Jesus described here (see verses 11–16)? How does this second advent differ from his first coming?

_____

_____

_____

_____

9. What happens to the Antichrist and his false prophet (v. 20)?

_____

_____

_____

But, wait—it gets even better, even more exciting. Keep reading on into Revelation 20!

> *Then I saw an angel come down from heaven with the key to the bottomless pit and a heavy chain in his hand. He seized the dragon—that old serpent, the Devil, Satan—and bound him in chains for a thousand years. The angel threw him into the bottomless pit, which he then shut and locked so Satan could not deceive the nations anymore until the thousand years were finished. Afterward he would be released again for a little while.*
>
> *Then I saw thrones, and the people sitting on them had been given the authority to judge. And I saw the souls of those who had been beheaded for their testimony about Jesus, for proclaiming the word of God. And I saw the souls of those who had not worshiped the beast or his statue, nor accepted his mark on their forehead or their hands. They came to life again, and they reigned with Christ for a thousand years. This is the first resurrection. (The rest of the dead did not come back to life until the thousand years had ended.) Blessed and holy are those who share in the first resurrection. For them the second death holds no power, but they will be priests of God and of Christ and will reign with him a thousand years.*
>
> *When the thousand years end, Satan will be let out of his prison. He will go out to deceive the nations from every corner of the earth, which are called Gog and Magog. He will gather them together for battle—a mighty host, as numberless as sand along the shore. And I saw them as they went up on the broad plain of the earth and surrounded God's people and the beloved city. But fire from heaven came down on the attacking armies and consumed them.*
>
> *Then the Devil, who betrayed them, was thrown into the lake of fire that burns with sulfur, joining the beast and the false prophet. There they will be tormented day and night forever and ever.* (Revelation 20:1–10)

10. How long is Satan in the bottomless pit?

_____

_____

_____

11. Why do you think God allows Satan out of his "prison" (v. 7)? What happens to him after that?

_____

_____

_____

_____

"People have asked the question why Satan will be loosed from his prison after the 1,000 years. This action is in keeping with God's purpose to demonstrate in history that man left to his own devices will, nevertheless, sin against God. Even though the Millennium provided a perfect environment for humanity with abundant revelation of God's power, the evil heart of man is manifest in the fact that people reject Christ and follow Satan when he is loosed. The loosing of Satan also is a demonstration of the wickedness of Satan and the fallen angels and how even 1,000 years in confinement does not change this."[1]

John Walvoord

Hell? Yes!

The Bible uses a variety of terms to speak of the place where the unrepentant are punished after death:

Sheol—a Hebrew word found often in the Old Testament and used broadly to mean "the place of the dead." As Charles Ryrie has noted, it is "a place of horror (Psalm 30:9; Numbers 16:33), weeping (Isaiah 38:3), and punishment (Job 24:19)."[2]

Hades—the Greek equivalent of Sheol, where unsaved people go to await the final judgment. This "temporary holding tank" will eventually be thrown lock, stock, and barrel into hell (Revelation 20:14 NIV).

Gehenna (2 Kings 23:10; Matthew 10:28)—an allusion to the valley of Hinnom, a stench-filled dumping ground where refuse was burned near Jerusalem, a picture of the lake of fire.

Lake of fire—a synonym for hell.

The bottomless pit or the Abyss—apparently a special "prison" in hell where some demons and evil spirits are held (see Luke 8:31; also 2 Peter 2:4).

12. How would you describe hell to someone who asked you what you believe about it?

_____

_____

_____

13. Why would a strong desire to escape the wrath to come be a good starting point to seek salvation in Christ?

_____

_____

_____

_____

"Think of the tyrants and dictators of history who have caused the deaths of millions of people. Think of mass murderers, child molesters, rapists, and others who have taken evil to its very depths. When a criminal commits an especially heinous crime and comes up for trial, it's common to hear people say things like, 'If there isn't a hell, there ought to be for a person like this.'

"It's interesting that even non-Christians recognize that certain people's sins are so bad they deserve to suffer forever for what they did. Of course, human justice is relative. But God's justice is absolute, and he takes our choices very seriously because people are very important in his sight.

"So let's affirm again what the Bible teaches. People go to hell because they choose to reject God and hold on to their sin, not because he just decides to send them there."[3]

Tony Evans

Finding the Connection

In *Desecration*, Buck reminded himself and Tsion reminded his fellow believers of the destiny of the beast, and of the ultimate victory of Jesus Christ. This is not "wishful thinking" or "pie-in-the-sky" optimism. It is raw truth. It is the ultimate hope of those who live in an evil world.

Right now it often seems as though the devil has the upper hand. It seems like evil is winning. Sometimes we wonder why God hasn't acted; why he hasn't intervened. The key word to remember is "yet." He hasn't stepped in *yet*. When enough people have repented and when evil has run its course, then, in the words of an old country preacher, "Christ will step out of heaven with that big ring of keys swinging from his belt, and he will say, 'Gentlemen, it's closing time.' "

14. How are you *comforted* by the closing chapters of Revelation?

_____

_____

15. How are you *motivated* by those same chapters? What do these truths make you want to go out and "do"?

_____

_____

_____

Revelation 5:6–14 gives us a peek into heaven. It is, so to speak, the "control center of the universe." Soak up the victory scene as described by the apostle John:

> I looked and I saw a Lamb that had been killed but was now standing between the throne and the four living beings and among the twenty-four elders. He had seven horns and seven eyes, which are the seven spirits of God that are sent out into every part of the earth. He stepped forward and took the scroll from the right hand of the one sitting on the throne. And as he took the scroll, the four living beings and the twenty-four elders fell down before the Lamb. Each one had a harp, and they held gold bowls filled with incense—the prayers of God's people!
>
> And they sang a new song with these words: "You are worthy to take the scroll and break its seals and open it. For you were killed, and your blood has ransomed people for God from every tribe and language and people and nation. And you have caused them to become God's kingdom and his priests. And they will reign on the earth."
>
> Then I looked again, and I heard the singing of thousands and millions of angels around the throne and the living beings and the elders. And they sang in a mighty chorus: "The Lamb is worthy—the Lamb who was killed. He is worthy to receive power and riches and wisdom and strength and honor and glory and blessing."
>
> And then I heard every creature in heaven and on earth and under the earth and in the sea. They also sang: "Blessing and honor and glory and power belong to the one sitting on the throne and to the Lamb forever and ever."

And the four living beings said, "Amen!" And the twenty-four elders fell down and worshiped God and the Lamb.

16. In these verses, to what degree do the inhabitants of heaven seem worried about the antics of Antichrist or stirred up about the schemes of Satan? Who is in control?

_____

_____

_____

17. Where, to what end, is the universe headed?

_____

_____

18. How does this heavenly vantage point affect the typical idea that the end of the world seems like a scary mystery?

_____

_____

_____

Biblical Descriptions of Hell

A place of outer darkness (Matthew 8:12)

A place full of rebellious creatures—human and angelic (Revelation 21:15)

A place of judgment (Hebrews 6:2) and punishment (Matthew 25:46)

A place of torment (Luke 16:24; Revelation 20:10)

An eternal place (Matthew 25:46; Revelation 14:11)

---

19. The items listed here that describe hell are not contradictory; they simply describe different aspects of hell that make it everyone's worst nightmare. Which of the descriptions captures what you would consider most dreadful about hell?

_____

_____

_____

20. Why do you think there is so little serious consideration of hell in sermons and in conversation among Christians today?

_____

_____

"There isn't much that can be said to brighten the picture or lessen the reality of hell. We need to know what hell will be like. We need to grasp the awful, eternal consequences of rejecting Christ so that we make sure we escape this place of suffering through faith in Christ, and make sure that, as much as it lies in our power, no one we know will have to experience God's eternal wrath on sin. God has done everything necessary to keep anyone from going to hell. He has an 'anti-hell' vaccine, the blood of Christ, available to all who trust Christ alone for their eternal salvation."[4]

Tony Evans

Making the Change

In the first paragraph of Exodus 23, a passage revealing God's standards for honesty, integrity, and justice, we find this verse:

> Do not join a crowd that intends to do evil. When you are on the witness stand, do not be swayed in your testimony by the opinion of the majority. (Exodus 23:2)

It's a good reminder that truth isn't determined by counting heads. Just because something is popular doesn't make it right. Sometimes a majority simply means most of the people are on the wrong side.

Christians are called to go against the flow of a culture that is running away from God. We have to stand against that current. When we do, our lives and words will attract the wrath of a world blinded by evil and living in darkness.

Remember what the apostle Paul told his protégé Timothy:

> You know how much persecution and suffering I have endured. You know all about how I was persecuted in Antioch, Iconium, and Lystra—but the Lord delivered me from all of it. (2 Timothy 3:11)

Then note the next statement Paul makes:

Yes, and everyone who wants to live a godly life in Christ Jesus will suffer persecution.
(2 Timothy 3:12)

Did you catch that? It's a *promise!* Not the sort of Bible promise most Christians cross-stitch and frame and put above the sofa but a promise just the same.

21. In what ways are you catching any heat for your faith? If not, why do you think?

   _____

   _____

   _____

22. What people has God put in your life who still haven't acknowledged Christ as Savior and Lord?

   _____

   _____

23. At the end of the previous lesson, you chose two people with whom to have a conversation. How did that go? What are some specific ways you could engage them further in a discussion about spiritual matters?

   _____

   _____

   _____

Pursuing the Truth

24. Why do Christians absolutely not have to fear the end of the world?

   _____

   _____

Romans 16:20 says:

The God of peace will soon crush Satan under your feet. May the grace of our Lord Jesus Christ be with you.

25. What is the promise here? How does this verse encourage you?

_____

_____

_____

NO WORRIES

"The story is told of a humble Bible-believing custodian at a liberal seminary who was waiting for the students to fin-ish a pickup basketball game so he could dust the gym floor. While the custodian was reading his Bible, one of these future ministers saw him and asked what he was reading. 'Revelation,' he replied. The young man, who evidently didn't believe anyone could understand prophecy–particularly a man who had never graduated from high school–asked, 'Do you understand what you are reading?'

" 'I sure do!' the man replied.

"Surprised at his answer, the seminarian asked, 'What does it say?'

"With a triumphant smile, the custodian declared, 'Jesus wins!' " [5]

Tim LaHaye and Jerry B. Jenkins

Lesson in Review . . .

- At the end of the Tribulation, Jesus Christ will return—an event known as the Glorious Appearing—and defeat his satanic enemies at the great and terrible Battle of Armageddon.
- The beast and the false prophet will be thrown into the lake of fire; the dragon, Satan, will be bound and cast into the bottomless pit for a thousand years while Christ rules the earth (the Millennium).
- At the end of the Millennium, Satan will be loosed one last time and will deceive some of the inhabitants of the earth.
- This will be his "last hurrah." Following this final rebellion, Satan and all his evil follow-ers will be cast into the lake of fire (hell), joining the Antichrist and the false prophet for all eternity.

Endnotes

Lesson 1: The Dragon—the Power Behind the Beast

1. Erwin Lutzer, "When All Hell Breaks Loose," in *Prophecy in Light of Today,* ed. Charles H. Dyer (Chicago: Moody, 2002), 72–73.
2. Quoted in Tim LaHaye and Jerry B. Jenkins, *Are We Living in the End Times?* (Wheaton: Tyndale House, 1999), 364.
3. Ibid., 264.
4. Ibid., 268–69.
5. C. S. Lewis, *The Screwtape Letters* (West Chicago, Ill.: Lord and King Associates, 1976), 9.
6. Lutzer, "When All Hell Breaks Loose," 73.
7. LaHaye and Jenkins, *Are We Living in the End Times?* 269–70.

Lesson 2: The Rise of the Beast

1. Tony Evans, *The Best Is Yet to Come* (Chicago: Moody, 2000), 174.
2. Ibid., 181.
3. Erwin Lutzer, "When All Hell Breaks Loose," in *Prophecy in Light of Today,* ed. Charles H. Dyer (Chicago: Moody, 2002), 77.
4. Evans, *The Best Is Yet to Come,* 181.

Lesson 3: The Character of the Beast

1. Tony Evans, *The Best Is Yet to Come* (Chicago: Moody, 2000), 176.
2. Erwin Lutzer, "When All Hell Breaks Loose," in *Prophecy in Light of Today,* ed. Charles H. Dyer (Chicago: Moody, 2002), 72.
3. Charles Ryrie, *A Survey of Bible Doctrine* (Chicago: Moody, 1972), 79.
4. Tim LaHaye and Jerry B. Jenkins, *Are We Living in the End Times?* (Wheaton: Tyndale House, 1999), 288.

Lesson 4: The Beast's Assistant

1. Charles Ryrie, *The Ryrie Study Bible* (Chicago: Moody, 1976, 1978), 1911.
2. Tim LaHaye and Jerry B. Jenkins, *Are We Living in the End Times?* (Wheaton: Tyndale House, 1999), 285.
3. Tony Evans, *The Best Is Yet to Come* (Chicago: Moody, 2000), 182.
4. LaHaye and Jenkins, *Are We Living in the End Times?* 289.

Lesson 5: The Résumé of the Beast

1. Charles H. Dyer, "A Peace to End All Peace," in *Prophecy in Light of Today*, ed. Charles H. Dyer (Chicago: Moody, 2002), 31.
2. Tony Evans, *The Best Is Yet to Come* (Chicago: Moody, 2000), 175.
3. Ibid., 175–76.
4. Charles Ryrie, *Basic Theology* (Chicago: Moody, 1999), 550.
5. Dyer, "A Peace to End All Peace," 31.
6. Ryrie, *Basic Theology*, 556.

Lesson 6: Damned! The Destiny of the Beast

1. John Walvoord, *The Prophecy Knowledge Handbook* (Dallas: Dallas Seminary Press, 1990), 629.
2. Charles Ryrie, *A Survey of Bible Doctrine* (Chicago: Moody, 1972), 184.
3. Tony Evans, *The Best Is Yet to Come* (Chicago: Moody, 2000), 293.
4. Ibid., 304–5.
5. Tim LaHaye and Jerry B. Jenkins, *Are We Living in the End Times?* (Wheaton: Tyndale House, 1999), 241.

SINCE 1894, Moody Publishers has been dedicated to equip and motivate people to advance the cause of Christ by publishing evangelical Christian literature and other media for all ages, around the world. Because we are a ministry of the Moody Bible Institute of Chicago, a portion of the proceeds from the sale of this book go to train the next generation of Christian leaders.

If we may serve you in any way in your spiritual journey toward understanding Christ and the Christian life, please contact us at www.moodypublishers.com.

"All Scripture is God-breathed and is useful for teaching, rebuking, correcting and training in righteousness, so that the man of God may be thoroughly equipped for every good work."
—2 TIMOTHY 3:16, 17